# COUNTRY PATCHWORK & QUILTING

## By Leslie Linsley

*Photographs by Jon Aron*

**Sedgewood® Press**
New York, N.Y.

## Dedication

For my grandmother, Anna Zuckerman,
and my mother, Ruth Linsley,
who encouraged the kind of creativity
that has led to a most satisfying way of life.

**Illustrations:**
Peter Peluso, Jr.
Robby Smith

**Craft contributors:**
Ginnie Beaulieu
Margaret Detmer
Helen Jenkins
Susan Fernald Joyce
Ruth Linsley
Peter Peluso, Jr.
Robby Smith

Homespun Fabric by Waverly, a division of Schumacher & Co., Inc.

All projects are quilted or stuffed with Poly-Fil from Fairfield Processing Corporation

Fabric dye and color remover from Rit Dye

**For Sedgewood® Press:**
Director: Elizabeth P. Rice
Project Editor: Sandy Towers
Production Manager: Bill Rose
Design: Remo Cosentino/Bookgraphics

Distributed by Meredith Corporation
ISBN: 0-696-02301-6
Library of Congress Catalog Card Number: 87-063528
Printed in the United States of America
10  9  8  7  6  5  4  3  2  1

# Contents

# Introduction

**I**n the past few years, I've written 4 books on quilting, gone to numerous quilt shows, collected a fairly extensive library on the subject, and talked to countless quilters. Quilting has become, once again, a full-blown American craft. I say "once again" because quilting has always been an American tradition, but every few years it becomes a craze, a trend, a way of life. So much so that the media picks up on it and suddenly the papers report every quilting event, magazines are not complete without a quilt project each month, and every city and town announces a quilting club activity. In fact, craft shops once devoted to other crafts are suddenly "quilt shops" exclusively.

Quilting has always been with the American people. We pieced fabric together for purposes of keeping warm in colonial days and formed quilting bees in order to socialize while being productive. Today's quilting clubs are very much the same. Church members have long formed groups in order to make fund-raising quilts to raffle off. We have 4-H clubs and Homemakers' Extension groups that include quilting as one of their main activities. We have quilting bees with only a few members and national quilters' organizations with hundreds of members. Quilting is being taught in grade school as well as high-school home-economics classes. There are books and home-learning tapes about how to do patchwork, appliqué, and other quilting techniques. Quilters' magazines abound. There are mail-order sources for everything needed to make a quilt. Whether you live in a rural area or a big city, there's a good chance that you'll find a number of avid quilters eager for regular quilting get-togethers.

When New York City was hosting the Statue of Liberty's hundredth birthday celebration, one of the major attractions of the event was the Great American Quilt Festival. Quilters from all over the country worked for months making quilts to commemorate the Statue. The Museum of American Folk Art, along with The National Needlework Association (TNNA), sponsored another quilting extravaganza. This was a 1,000-foot quilted banner called *From Sea To Shining Sea*.

Thousands of enthusiastic quilters, from beginners to very experienced stitchers, donated hundreds of hours each to the making of 3-foot squares representing their states. Three hundred and fifty squares were stitched together to make up this fascinating project, which then went on to tour the country and has been viewed by millions. What a wonderful tribute to our American quilting tradition and our American people! It is a statement that quilting is appreciated as our own indigenous craft and that we want to keep the tradition alive.

One of the many women whom I interviewed while I was involved in that project was a member of an Indiana Homemakers' Group. A proud American, she voiced the feeling of the group, and it is one I've heard expressed over and over again. She said, "I remember as a young girl sitting under the dining-room table and listening to my mother and her sisters (my aunts) talking. It was my private house, because they were working on a quilt and the fabric was spread over the table and spilled down onto the floor. They never knew I was there. Later, when I was old enough, they let me thread the needles for them so they wouldn't have to stop what they were doing. I remember how proud I was when I was able to join that group of women to make a quilt for the church raffle. Today, as a fourth-generation quilter, I feel so proud and lucky to have such a fine heritage. It is one that I am now passing on to my daughters, and even my son has begun to get interested. I dream of quilt patterns and know that I will never live long enough to complete every project I've dreamed up."

And from another quilter in Kentucky: "I love the words to our national anthem and tried to incorporate them into my quilt. It is such a wonderful thing to be able to honor our country and the Statue of Liberty in such a personal way." One of the quilters I met was a Native American. She said, "I always have a quilting square in my lap. Quilting is part of my life. Everything I do, every major event, is commemorated in my quilts. When my children leave home to begin their new lives without me, I want them to take a piece of their past with them, and this will be in the form of a quilt."

When I was a child, we always had quilts on the beds. The older, non-salvageable quilts were cut up and made into pillows. Now my daughters have some of these quilts and a pillow or two. I can even point out the patches that were made from my outgrown childhood clothes, which my mother used to refurbish those quilts. Someday, my grandchildren will reach into the attic and find one of those heirloom quilts, and I'll tell them how and when each patch was made and all about their family history, so lovingly stitched into the fabric.

When I begin a new book, I am excited immediately. I love the prospect of creating a whole new batch of projects for the purpose of teaching a craft. I love the challenge of designing projects small enough to finish quickly so that no one becomes discouraged, yet can feel that each new project moves the learning process along. My husband and partner, Jon Aron, and I usually start by making a list of everything we think you, the reader, should know about the craft. And then we begin to outline the various projects that you can make, using your skills in ascending order. We try to make sure that the projects will interest an experienced crafter as well as a beginner. This means that while a project may be easy to do, the end result will be worth your time. We like to think that we've presented a good variety of quick-and-easy projects, not just for the beginner, but for the more accomplished quilter. We know that everyone is busy. We also know that our readers like time-consuming projects that are worth the effort. We often hear from working women who prefer a project that can be worked on over a period of months, rather than a small project to finish in an evening. This book holds something for every time frame. While making the small gifts, you will learn the various quilting techniques that will enable you to make some of the pillows, table coverings, and quilts that take a bit longer. Because we know that weekend quilts are so popular, we've designed a new quilt that can be pieced in a weekend. It is a traditional Amish design in an up-to-date look. The avid quilter who wants to spend more time can quilt by hand to make a truly beautiful keepsake or special gift.

I interviewed two quilters living in my home town, Nantucket Island, Massachusetts. They are typical of today's young women, juggling home, career, marriage, and parenting. They also find time for quilt-making. Susan Fernald Joyce's specialty is the small wall hanging, and she especially likes the Around the World design. She exhibits her work at a local art gallery, is often commissioned to do one-of-a-kind projects, and teaches an adult-education class in quilting. She and her husband, Nelson, have one young son, Russell, who keeps them running. But Susan often finds time to collaborate on a quilt project with her friend Margaret Detmer. Last year, the two women made several quilts for the annual craft show, and together they made the Schoolhouse Wall Hanging on page 65. Maggie recently taught a quilting class at her son Jody's grammar school. The children created the designs on their squares with fabric crayons. Then each took a turn at the sewing machine that was set up in the classroom. "They absolutely loved it," Maggie told me, while Jody beamed with pride and his 2-year-old sister Emma Jane vied for attention. "I taught the children all about the quilting steps and the background of quilting and they were fascinated. They couldn't wait to get at the sewing machine," Maggie added. You might think of doing a similar project in your community.

One day, Susan brought me an old quilt that had been given to her because it needed repairs. It was made from hundreds of bright fabric scraps. Since everyone who sews has pieces of fabric in a scrap basket,

I thought it would be a good project to include here. Most scraps are too small to make anything significant, but we all keep them, sure that someday they will be needed and appreciated. My daughter Robby, who works with us and is an expert quilter, figured out the directions for making this wonderful heirloom quilt. This quilt gave us the idea of finding more antique quilts that you might like to make. There are lots of old quilts available in antique shops and, if one searches, in people's homes. We wanted to find quilts that were of particular interest and in good condition. They had to be do-able as well. One such quilt was a contemporary-looking version of the traditional design called Drunkard's Path. We had never before seen this interpretation, done in red and white to form large polka dots. It is quite dramatic as a wall hanging in a modern home, proving once again that the graphic quality of early patchwork quilts is amazingly contemporary. This is one of the more difficult projects in this book, and I advise starting with some of the small gifts before attempting such an ambitious project.

Take the time to read the material at the beginning of the book before starting a project. It will give you a grasp of quilting processes and probably save you time by preventing errors. From time to time, you can refer back to specific information when the directions for a particular project suggest doing so. In this way each set of project directions won't seem out of context.

Leslie Linsley

# Quilting Terms

As with other crafts, quilting has a "language" of its own. It is easily learned and will help you to understand the different processes and the different kinds of quilts. When you look at a patchwork or appliquéd quilt, for example, you'll have a good idea how it was made. This information will also help you understand quiltmaking directions. Quilting terms are basic and logical.

*Appliqué.* The technique of creating a design by cutting a shape from one fabric and stitching it, either by hand or by machine, to a contrasting fabric background.

*Backing.* The piece of fabric used on the underside of the pieced or appliquéd top. Usually, backing is made of fabric of the same weight as the top. It may be made from solid or printed fabric to match the top design. Sometimes the backing is made from the same fabric as that used to create the borders on the quilt top. I especially like to use an old sheet for the backing. Sheet sizes are large enough not to need piecing, and an old sheet is nice and soft.

*Basting.* Securing the top, batting, and backing together with long, loose stitches before quilting. These stitches are removed after each section is quilted.

*Batting.* The soft lining that makes the quilt puffy and gives it warmth. Batting comes in various thicknesses, each appropriate for different kinds of projects. It may be made of cotton or polyester, or a blend of the two. Batting also comes in small, fluffy pieces that are used for stuffing projects such as sachets, pincushions, or pillows.

*Binding.* The way the raw edges of fabric are finished. Many quilters cut the backing slightly larger than the top piece so they can bring the extra fabric forward to finish the edges. Contrasting fabric or bias binding is also used.

*Block.* Geometric or symmetrical pieces of fabric sewn together to create a design. The finished blocks are sewn together to create the finished quilt top. Another word for *block* is *square.*

*Borders.* Fabric strips that frame the top design. Borders may be narrow or wide. A quilt may have one border or more around the center design. Borders are sometimes made from one of the fabrics used in the blocks or center design, or from a contrasting fabric. Borders are often used to extend the size of a quilt top so that it drops down over the sides of a mattress.

Traditionally, quilting designs are stitched in the borders to add interest. Nowadays many quilters leave this area free of stitches in order to complete the project more quickly.

*Patchwork.*  Fabric pieces sewn together, to create an overall design. Sometimes the pieces form geometric blocks that are then sewn together to make up the completed quilt.

*Piecing.*  Joining patchwork pieces together to form a design on the block.

*Quilting.*  Stitching together two layers of fabric with a layer of batting between.

*Quilting patterns.*  The lines or markings on the fabric that make up the design. Quilt along these lines, with small hand or machine stitches, which might be straight or curved or made up of elaborate curlicued patterns. Small quilting stitches can also follow the seam lines where pieces of fabric are joined. Or a quilting design can be created by stitching a grid of diamonds over the entire fabric.

*Sash or lattice strips.*  Narrow pieces of fabric used to frame the individual blocks and join them together. They are often created in a complementary color.

*Setting.*  Joining quilt blocks to form the finished quilt top.

*Template.*  A stiff full-size pattern shape used to trace the pattern elements onto fabric. It can be cut from cardboard or plastic. Some quilters make sandpaper templates because they are the right weight and won't slide on the fabric. When cutting the fabric, you will usually add ¼ inch for seam allowance. When any project in this book calls for a template, the instructions will state whether seam allowance is included.

*Top.*  The front layer of a quilt with the right side showing. Patchwork or appliquéd pieces create the top fabric.

## Materials for Quilting

*Fabric.*  You can never have too many different fabrics to choose from when designing a quilting project. Fabric is the main concern: what kind, how much and what colors or prints will work together.

Almost every kind of fabric has been used for making quilts and quilt projects. However, most quilters prefer cotton and, if necessary, will settle for a cotton/polyester blend in order to find the right color or pattern for the project. Pure cotton should be washed before it is used. This removes any sizing in the fabric and allows for shrinkage.

In order to create old-looking patchwork, Jon and I tried to fade some bright colors. We filled the sink with water and plenty of fabric bleach and soaked the red fabrics. When we removed, rinsed, and dried them, they were as bright as before. We've discovered that it is not easy to fade colorfast fabrics. There is a color-removing product available that is effective if used carefully (in order not to remove *all* color). If this process interests you, experiment with scraps.

If you'd like to dye fabrics in order to create just the desired shades of color, try experimenting with fabric dyes. This is a great way to graduate color for a Sunshine and Shadow quilt. Read the directions on the package and test colors with scraps of fabric, timing each piece left in the dye bath in order to achieve the desired shades.

When you're collecting a variety of fabric prints for your quilting projects, it's a good idea to have a selection of lights and darks. The colors and patterns of the fabric will greatly affect the design. Calico has always been used for quilting projects. The small, overall prints can be used effectively together, and there is a wide variety of colors to choose from.

*Batting.* The filler for a quilted fabric is usually called quilt batting or fiber fill; it is a layer of fibers used between the top fabric and backing. Although it is lightweight and airy, it gives the quilted fabric bulk and warmth. You can find this prepackaged or sold by the yard in most fabric stores, five and tens, and notion stores. It comes in various thicknesses for different uses. Often I will list thin quilt batting as the material of choice for a specific project. Most packaged batting will state on the label what the thickness is most suitable for, such as a quilted jacket or warm bed quilt. With this information, you can buy the best batting for your project. Most batting is of medium thickness and works well for the majority of projects. Therefore different thicknesses aren't a real concern. Unless project instructions specifically state otherwise, use the medium thickness.

When quilting is done, the batting is secured to the back of the top fabric. Sometimes the quilting is done right through the backing material as well. The quilting threads are stitched through the layers of material to achieve the three-dimensional effect of quilting. I like the polyblend filler the best. All the women I know who quilt agree. The cotton batting is especially difficult to stitch through and I rarely recommend it.

*Needles.* All of the projects in this book are stitched on a sewing machine. The quilting can be done by hand or on the machine. If stitching by hand, you will need #7 or #8 sharps, which are the most common needle sizes used for hand-quilting. They are often called "betweens."

*Thread.* Match the thread to the color of the fabric. Cotton-blend thread is best for appliqué and piecing.

*Scissors.* Good-quality scissors can't be beat! They are essential for accurately cutting your fabric. *Do not use your fabric scissors for cutting paper.* Doing this will ruin your scissors.

*Thimble.* When quilting, I always start out with a thimble, and in fewer than 4 stitches I've abandoned it. I know that if I got used to wearing it my life would be a lot easier, or safer, but I can't. If you are making a project with hand-sewn stitches, you will be taking 3 to 6 stitches at a time through 3 layers of fabric. A thimble can make this task more fun and painless. It's up to you.

*Templates.* Shirt cardboard or manila oaktag used for filing folders is ideal for templates. Acetate is a good material, too, because you'll get clean, crisp edges, and you can see through it. Templates will be used for appliqué pieces when a repeat design is required. If you are cutting one design, you can simply pin the paper pattern to the fabric to use as a cutting guide.

*Markers.* Sometimes a pattern or design has to be traced from the book and transferred to the fabric. When you want an overall quilting design, you'll need lines to follow. A soft pencil is good for these purposes. Some quilters use a water-soluble marker to transfer quilting lines onto their fabrics and then remove the lines with a mister after stitching. Be sure to follow the manufacturer's instructions carefully, and test the marker on a scrap of fabric before you start your project.

*Iron.* Have you ever known anyone to sew without an iron next to the sewing machine? It's impossible to be without it. If you are doing patchwork, it's handy to pad a stool or chair with a piece of batting and place it next to you, alongside the sewing machine. As you piece the fabric, you can iron the seams without getting up. Use a steam setting.

*Cutting board.* This is a handy item for the quick measuring and cutting you'll use when making quilts. It is available in fabric stores or from mail-order sources.

*Ruler and yardstick.* These are musts. A metal ruler can be used as a straightedge for the most accurate cutting. Use the yardstick for cutting lengths of fabric when you must mark and cut at least 36 inches at one time. The width of the yardstick is often used to mark a grid pattern for quilting. You simply draw the first line, then flip the yardstick over and continue to mark lines without ever removing the yardstick from the fabric. You will have a perfect 1-inch grid.

# Quilting Techniques

## ESTIMATING FABRIC AMOUNTS

All fabric used for these projects is 45 inches wide. All measurements are figured with a ¼-inch seam allowance.

When estimating yardage for a bed quilt, measure your bed fully made. This means with bed pad, sheets, and blankets over the mattress. Measure the length, width, and depth, including the box spring. Decide if you want a slight overhang, an overhang with a dust ruffle, or a drop to the floor, and whether or not the quilt will extend up and over the pillows. If a quilt size for any project shown in this book isn't the exact size for your bed, it can be changed by adding to, or subtracting from, the border measurements. Doing this shouldn't change the basic design.

## PIECING THE BACKING

You may have to piece panels together for the back of a quilt, tablecloth, or wall hanging in order to get the correct size. Use the full width of fabric, usually 45 inches, cut to the appropriate length. Cut another piece the same size. Then cut the second strip of fabric in half lengthwise so you have 2 narrow strips the same size. Join each of these 2 matching panels to each long side edge of the full, center panel to avoid a seam down the middle of the quilt backing. Press seams open.

## ENLARGING DESIGNS

Most patterns and designs are shown full-size, but sometimes they are too large to fit on a page. When this is the case, the designs are shown on a grid. Each square on the grid equals 1 inch. This means that you will transfer or copy the design onto graph paper marked with 1-inch squares. Begin by counting the number of squares on the pattern in the book. Number them horizontally and again vertically. Count the same number of squares on your larger graph and number them in the same way. Copy the design onto your grid one square at a time.

## TRANSFERRING A LARGE DESIGN

Trace the pattern pieces or quilting design from the book. Place a piece of dressmaker's tracing (carbon) paper on the right side of the fabric with the carbon side down and tracing paper on top. Go over all pattern lines with a tracing wheel or ballpoint pen to transfer the design. Remove the carbon and tracing paper.

## MAKING A TEMPLATE

Transfer the pattern to the template material by first tracing the outline. Place the tracing face down on the cardboard and rub over each traced line. The outline will come off on the cardboard. Remove the tracing and go over the lines with a ballpoint pen to make them legible. Cut out the design outline from the cardboard. If you are using acetate, simply place it over the tracing and cut out the exact shape.

Determine which template will be used for each fabric. Place the templates ½ inch apart to allow for the ¼-inch seam allowance when cutting out each piece. You may even want to allow for ⅜-inch seams for easy turning of the edges. This will be determined by the thickness of the fabric, whether or not the design has points or curves, and so on. Try it both ways to see which works best for you. Consider the grain of the fabric and the direction of the print when placing your templates.

## SEWING POINTS

Many traditional quilt patterns are created from triangles, diamonds, or similar shapes. The points present a challenge and require special care.

When stitching 2 such pieces together, sew along the stitch line, but do not sew into the seam allowance at each point (see Figure 1). It helps to mark the finished points with a pin so you can begin and end your seam at these marks.

Figure 1. Sewing Points

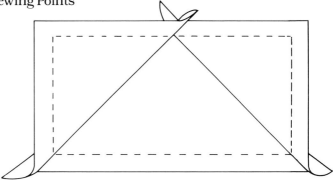

## SEWING CURVES

Before turning a curved appliqué, stay-stitch (loose stitches) along the seam line, then clip or notch evenly spaced cuts along the edge in the seam allowance. Clip all inward curves and notch all outward curves. When the fabric is turned under, it will lie flat.

## SEWING INSIDE CORNER EDGE

Place a pin across the point of the stitches and clip up to the stitches in the seam allowance in order to turn the fabric under.

## SEWING OUTSIDE CORNER EDGE

Once you've stitched around a corner, clip off half the seam allowance across the point. Turn fabric back, press seams open, and trim excess fabric away.

## TURNING CORNERS

It's often a bit difficult to turn corners and continue a seam line. Figure 1 shows the 3 pieces to be joined. With right sides facing, stitch piece A to piece B, as shown in Figure 2. Next, join C to A, as shown in Figure 3. Leave the needle down in the fabric. Lift the presser foot and clip the seam to the needle. Slide B under C and adjust so the edges of B align with C. Lower the presser foot and stitch along the seam line (see Figure 4).

Turning Corners

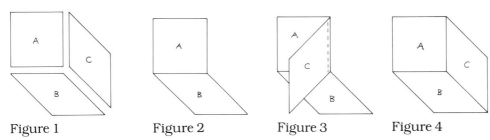

Figure 1          Figure 2          Figure 3          Figure 4

## APPLIQUE

*Hand-appliqué.* Using a template, cut out each pattern piece. If there is no seam allowance on your template, add ¼ to ⅜ inch all around when cutting. Place the template on the back of the fabric and press all edges over the template edges. If the appliqué is curved, clip all edges to seam line before turning.

Pin the appliqué in place on the background fabric and blindstitch or whipstitch it all around. The appliquéd fabric is then backed with batting before you quilt around the design. Use short running stitches around the inside edge of the appliqué.

*Machine-appliqué.* Cut the fabric without seam allowance. Edges need not be turned. Pin the appliqué in position on the fabric and zigzag-stitch around the edges.

## HOW TO QUILT

*Quilting* means sewing layers of fabric and batting together to produce a padded fabric held together by the stitching. It is often decorative and is generally the finishing step in appliqué and patchwork projects. The quilting is what makes a project interesting and gives it a textured look.

*Basting.*   Before quilting, you will baste the quilt top, batting, and backing together. To avoid a lump of filler at any point, begin at the center of the top and baste with long, loose stitches outward, creating a sunburst pattern. There should be about 6 inches between the basted lines at the edges of the quilt. Baste from the top only. These stitches will be cut away as you do your quilting.

*Hand-quilting.*   Thread your needle and knot one end as for regular hand-sewing. Bring it up through the back to the front and give the knotted end a good tug to pull it through the backing fabric into the batting. Keep your thread fairly short (about 18 inches) and take small running stitches. Follow your premarked quilting pattern.

*Machine-quilting.*   This is a quicker way to quilt, but does not produce the same rich look of authentic quilting that hand-stitching has. It is best to do it when the batting isn't too thick. The Weekend Quilt on page 99 was machine stitched in the channels of the seams to hold it together. Because this is a quick and easy quilt to piece, it is appropriate that the quilting be done quickly as well. As you can see, the absence of hand-stitching does not detract from this good-looking, contemporary version of an Amish design.

*Outlining.*   This is the method of quilting just outside the lines of your appliquéd designs or along the patchwork seams. With outlining, each design element is pronounced and the layers of fabric are secure.

*Overall quilting.* When you want to fill large areas of the background with quilting, choose a simple design. The background quilting should not interfere with the patchwork or appliqué elements.

Make grid patterns of squares or diamond shapes with a yardstick or masking tape for accurate spacing. For a quick-and-easy method, lay a yardstick diagonally across the fabric and mark it with a light pencil. Without removing the yardstick, turn it over and mark along the edge once again. Continue across the fabric. You should have perfect 1-inch spaces between each line. Lay the yardstick across the fabric at the opposite corner from where you began and repeat the process to create a 1-inch grid over the top of the fabric. Stitch along these lines. The stitching will hide the pencil lines.

# Quick-and-Easy Methods

## STRIP PIECING

This is the method by which you sew strips of different fabrics together and then cut them into units, which are then arranged to make up the entire quilt top. Rather than cutting and sewing individual squares together over and over again, you sew together 2 or more strips of fabric and then cut the sewn strip into segments that have exactly the same dimensions. These units are then arranged and pieced—stitched—together in different positions to form the quilt pattern.

## RIGHT TRIANGLES

There is a quick-and-easy way to join light and dark triangles to create squares of any size. Once you've determined the size of your finished square you add 1 inch to it. For example, if you want to create 2-inch squares, you will cut strips of light and dark fabric 3 inches wide by the length of your fabric, or the dimension given for each project.

Using your cutting board, place the 2 fabrics down with right sides facing up. Use your yardstick to draw a grid of 3-inch squares on the fabric.

Next, draw diagonal lines, as shown in Figure 1. Stitch a ¼-inch seam on each side of the diagonal lines, as shown.

Cut on all solid lines to get the individual units of light and dark (or contrasting fabric) triangles. Clip the corners, open, and press.

Figure 1. Right-Triangle Method

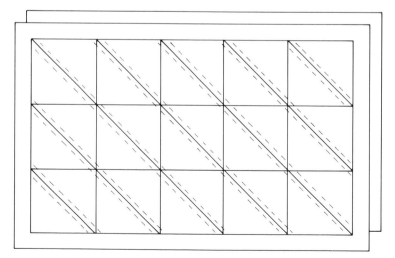

# Country Gifts

**W**hether it's a birthday, anniversary, or holiday, all of us anticipate gift-giving occasions. A handmade gift is always appreciated and usually cherished for its personal value. It is more fun to make a gift than to buy one. We can make something that suits personal tastes and give something of ourselves as well.

Country style has become so prevalent that it's a sure bet the country gift you make will fit right in with any decor. Pine-scented pillows to sweeten a closet, appliquéd kitchen towels, a basket of sachets, a patchwork-cat pillow and a year-round wreath are some of the easy-to-make projects here that can be finished in a couple of hours. I know that not everyone wants to tackle a month-long project each time they have the desire to make something, especially a gift item.

The projects in this section will give you the opportunity to try different quilting techniques. Almost all can be made from scraps of fabric that you have on hand, and the results will be far from ordinary.

# Country Potholders

These pastel potholders are made of pink-and-green plaid homespun fabric. Each 8 × 8 inch-potholder is pieced together in a different quilt pattern. You can make the potholders in colors to match your kitchen, since homespun comes in many colors. Homespun is a good fabric for these projects because it is heavier than most cottons, such as calico.

## Materials

small amounts of green plaid homespun

small amounts of solid coral homespun

8 × 16-inch piece of batting for each potholder

## POTHOLDER #1
### Directions

*Note:* All measurements include ¼-inch seam allowance.

*Cut the following:*

from green plaid: 4 rectangles, each 2½ × 4½ inches

from coral: 1 square, 4½ × 4½ inches

                    4 squares, each 2½ × 2½ inches

Figure 1

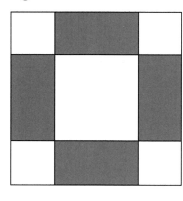

**1.** With right sides facing and raw edges aligned, stitch a small coral square to each short end of a green-plaid rectangle. Open seams and press. Repeat.

**2.** Next, stitch a green-plaid rectangle, along the long edge, to each side of 4½-inch coral square. Open seams and press.

**3.** With right sides facing and raw edges aligned, join rows together with the wide row between the 2 narrow rows, as shown in Figure 1.

**4.** See finishing directions on page 22.

## POTHOLDER #2
### Directions

Figure 2

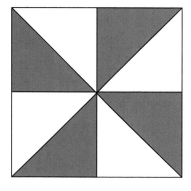

*Note:* All measurements include ¼-inch seam allowance.

*Cut the following:*

from green plaid: 2 squares, each 5 × 5 inches. Cut each square into 2 triangles.

from coral: 2 squares, each 5 × 5 inches. Cut each square into 2 triangles.

**1.** With right sides facing and raw edges aligned, stitch a green-plaid triangle to a coral triangle along the long edge. Repeat to make 4 green plaid-and-coral squares. Open seams and press.

**2.** Next, stitch squares together as shown in Figure 2. Open seams and press.

**3.** See finishing directions on page 22.

20

# POTHOLDER #3
## Directions

*Note:* All measurements include ¼-inch seam allowance.

*Cut the following:*

from green plaid: 1 square, 6⅛ × 6⅛ inches

from coral: 2 squares, each 5 × 5 inches. Cut each square into 2 triangles.

**Country Potholders**

Figure 3

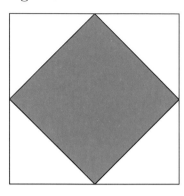

Figure 4

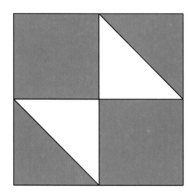

**1.** With right sides facing and raw edges aligned, stitch a coral triangle along the diagonal to each side of the green-plaid square, as shown in Figure 3. This makes a larger square.

**2.** Open seams and press.

**3.** See finishing directions below.

## POTHOLDER #4

### Directions

*Note:* All measurements include ¼-inch seam allowance.

*Cut the following:*

from green plaid: 1 square, 5 × 5 inches. Cut into 2 triangles.
       2 squares, each 5 × 5 inches

from coral: 1 square, 5 × 5 inches. Cut into 2 triangles.

**1.** With right sides facing and raw edges aligned, stitch a green-plaid triangle to a coral triangle along the long edge. Open seams and press. Repeat.

**2.** With right sides facing and raw edges aligned, stitch a green plaid-and-coral square to a green-plaid square. Open seams and press. Repeat with remaining 2 squares, as shown in Figure 4. Open seams and press.

*To finish*

**1.** Cut a strip, 1½ × 6 inches, from either fabric for hanging loop.

**2.** With wrong sides facing, fold in half lengthwise and press. Turn raw edges in ¼ inch and press. Stitch along the long edge.

**3.** Fold into a loop, overlapping the raw ends. Pin raw ends to one corner of the potholder so the loop lies on the front of the patchwork top.

**4.** Cut the batting in half so that you have 2 pieces, each 8 inches square. Cut a backing piece, 8½ × 8½ inches, from either fabric.

**5.** Pin one piece of batting to the back of the potholder top and quilt by hand or machine along all seam lines.

**6.** Pin the second piece of batting to the wrong side of the backing fabric.

**7.** With right sides facing and all edges aligned (hanging loop is between), stitch around 3 sides and 4 corners (making sure to catch the raw ends of the loop.) Turn right-side-out and push corners out with the eraser end of a pencil or with a crochet needle. Press.

**8.** Turn raw edges to inside and slip-stitch opening closed.

# Patchwork Cat

This 13-inch-high cat is made of 1-inch squares cut from light and dark, solid and printed fabrics. The backing is a solid piece cut from one of the fabrics used on the front. This is a good project to make with the tiny scraps left over from other projects. The quilting is done by hand in an overall grid pattern.

## Materials

assorted calico scraps
¼ yard muslin
calico fabric, 10 × 15 inches, for backing
stuffing
tracing paper

## Directions

*Note:* All measurements include ¼-inch seam allowance. You will need approximately 150 squares in order to have enough of a selection to arrange attractively.

*Cut the following:*

from assorted calicos: 80 squares, each 1½ × 1½ inches
from muslin: 70 squares, each 1½ × 1½ inches

**1.** With right sides facing and raw edges aligned, stitch a calico square to a muslin square along one edge. Open seams and press.

**2.** Continue to join squares in this way, alternating a calico square with a muslin square, until you have a row of 10 squares. Make 15 rows, 8 beginning and ending with a muslin square, and 7 beginning and ending with a calico square. Press seams to one side.

**3.** With right sides facing and raw edges aligned, join all rows so that contrasting squares alternate across and down. You will have a patchwork fabric that is approximately 10½ × 15 inches.

**4.** Enlarge the cat pattern (see page 13 for enlarging details). Transfer to tracing paper.

**5.** Pin the cat pattern face up to the right side of the patchwork fabric and cut out. Trace the tail and pin it to the remaining piece of patchwork. Cut out the cat and tail separately.

**6.** Pin each pattern face down on the right side of the solid calico fabric. Cut out.

*To make tail*

**1.** With right sides facing and raw edges aligned, stitch tail pieces together, leaving straight edge open for turning. Turn right-side-out and stuff tightly. It will help to use the eraser end of a pencil or a crochet hook to do this.

**2.** Pin the raw edges of the tail in position on the front of the patch-work cat.

**3.** With right sides facing and raw edges aligned, pin the backing to the front of the cat with the tail between. Stitch all around, leaving bottom end open.

**4.** Clip into seam allowance around all curves. Clip into corners before turning right-side-out. Press.

**5.** Stuff tightly. Turn raw edges to inside and slip-stitch opening closed.

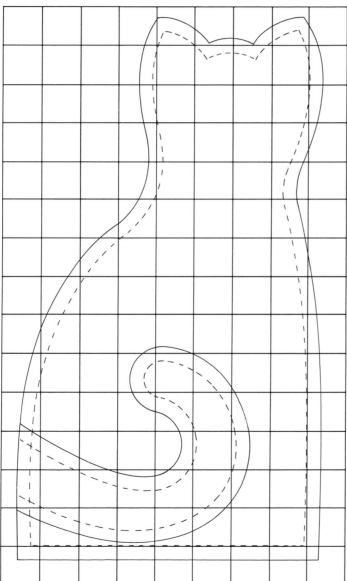

**Patchwork Cat**

Each square equals 1 inch

## Perfect Pin Pillows

You'll only need scraps of colored fabric to make these darling pin pillows. One is 4 inches square and made from strips of ¼-, ½-, and ¾-inch dark prints combined with muslin. The other is a 4½-inch square called Cathedral Window. This is a traditional quilt pattern sometimes called Stained Glass. It is made by folding squares of cloth to make "frames" for contrasting cloth "windows." Working on a tiny project is a good way to try your hand at this technique. If you find it satisfying, you might like to extend the process and make a pillow or a complete quilt like the one on page 131.

Small projects like these are excellent for practicing your quilting techniques before embarking on a larger project. The pincushions shown here were made by my mother, Ruth Linsley, when she was first learning to quilt. Now she is an expert quilter and you can see more of her fine work on the seat covers shown on page 60.

Figure 1

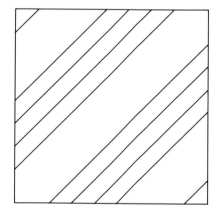

Figure 2

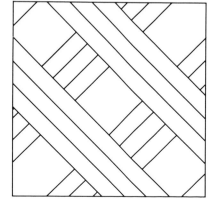

### Materials

fabric scraps

4½ × 4½-inch square muslin for striped pillow

4 squares, each 6½ × 6½ inches, of muslin for "cathedral window"

16 inches piping

stuffing

### STRIPED PIN PILLOW
### Directions

*Note:* All patchwork pieces were sewn with a zigzag stitch on the sewing machine. If you want to sew this project by hand, cut all your strips ¾ inch wide so that you'll have ¼ inch on each side edge for turning under.

**1.** Cut 12 strips of fabric, each ¼ × 4½ inches.

**2.** Arrange 2 sets of 3 strips each, with a ¾-inch space between, on 1 muslin square. (See Figure 1.) Pin in position, and trim the excess to the size of the muslin square. Pin a small strip across each of 2 diagonal corners.

**3.** Arrange 2 sets of 3 strips each to make a crisscross pattern, as shown in Figure 2.

**4.** Using a small zigzag stitch, sew along all edges of each fabric strip to attach it to muslin background.

**5.** Repeat steps 1 through 4 for back, or use a plain muslin square or colorful fabric for the backing.

*To finish*

**1.** With right sides facing and raw edges aligned, pin piping to patchwork top all around. Stitch around, as close to the cording as possible.

**2.** With right sides facing, pin backing to top. Turn work over, and, using the piping stitches as a guide, stitch around 3 sides and 4 corners.

**3.** Trim corners and turn right-side-out. Press.

**4.** Stuff, turn raw edges in, and slip-stitch opening closed.

## CATHEDRAL WINDOW PIN PILLOW
### Directions

**1.** Refer to Figure 1. Place a muslin square wrong-side up. Fold each side in ¼ inch and press.

**2.** Fold each corner in, to the center, as shown in Figures 1a and 1b. Sew the center points together by hand.

**3.** Next, fold the new corners in, to the center again, and secure firmly with a cross-stitch. (See Figures 1c and 1d). Make 4.

**4.** With right sides facing and raw edges aligned, join the 4 folded squares along one edge, using an overcast stitch to make a larger square.

**5.** Center a 1¾ × 1¾-inch colored fabric square over each overcast seam, with opposite points of colored fabric square on upper and lower ends of seam. Turn adjacent folded edges of the muslin squares toward the front, over the raw edges of the colored square. Stitch with a blind stitch. (See Figure 2.) Make each curve formed by turning the folded edges to the front identical to the others.

**6.** Fold each corner to the back center. Place a wad of stuffing on back. Fold corners over to the back again, enclosing the stuffing. Slip-stitch closed (see Figure 3).

Figure 1

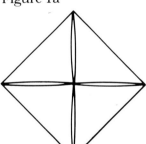

Figure 1a

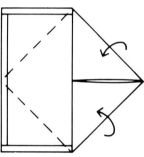

Figure 1b

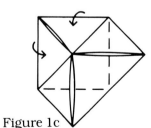

Figure 1c

Figure 1d

Figure 2

Figure 3

# Cookie-Cutter Appliqués

Simple shapes such as hearts and gingerbread men have always been used as country motifs for appliqué. I call these "cookie-cutter appliqués" because you can use your cookie cutters to make them. While I've provided you with the shapes in the exact sizes for these projects, you can take your designs for other items right from your kitchen drawer.

## PINE-SCENTED PILLOWS

These little pine-filled pillows can be tossed on the bed for sweet dreams or placed in the linen closet for sweet-smelling sheets and towels. They will also keep clothes closets fresh, and they look darling in a basket or as accents, placed with larger pillows on a chair or sofa.

They are made from blue-and-white ticking fabric or homespun, with red-and-white checks, plaids, or solids for the appliqués and piping. The largest pillow is $7 \times 11$ inches. The smaller ones are 6 inches square.

### Materials (for all 3 pillows)

¼ yard blue-and-white ticking

¼ yard red-checked homespun fabric

small scraps of solid red, red plaid, red-checked *or* calico fabric, each
    $4 \times 4$ inches

2½ yards cording *or* premade piping (1 package)

stuffing

pine needles *or* potpourri

tracing paper

### Directions

**1.** Cut 2 pieces of ticking, each $6\frac{1}{2} \times 6\frac{1}{2}$ inches. Cut 2 pieces of the same size from the red-checked fabric.

**2.** Cut 2 pieces of ticking, each $7\frac{1}{2} \times 11\frac{1}{2}$ inches.

*Note:* If you don't have a zigzag attachment on your sewing machine, cut each heart appliqué ¼ inch larger than pattern size all around. (See page 15 for hand-appliqué details.)

**3.** Trace the heart pattern (see page 32) and pin to the solid red scrap. Cut out. Repeat with the red plaid and then the red-checked or calico fabric.

**4.** Position and pin each heart shape on the top piece of each pillow fabric. They can be placed in the center, as I did with one small pillow, or in one corner, as shown with the others.

**5.** Using red thread and a narrow zigzag stitch on your sewing machine, stitch around the edges of each heart.

### To make piping

*Note:* Since these pillows are so small, you can find prepackaged piping in the right size for the projects. But you are limited to a few solid colors, one of which is red. I used red for the larger pillow, but wanted to use checks and stripes for the smaller ones. If you'd like to do the same, it is easy enough to make your own.

**1.** Cut a strip of fabric, $1\frac{1}{2} \times 25$ inches, for each small pillow and $1\frac{1}{2} \times 37$ inches for the larger pillow.

**2.** Encase cording between fabric, having cording and fabric ends even at the start. Stitch close to cording with your zipper foot. You will have an inch of fabric left over. Turn this raw end under slightly and press. You will use this to overlap the raw end when attaching to the pillow top.

*To finish*

**1.** With right sides facing and raw edges aligned, pin the piping around the edge of the pillow top, overlapping the ends. Stitch around, as close to the cording as possible.

**2.** With right sides facing and raw edges aligned, pin the backing to the pillow top with the piping between.

**3.** Turn the pillow over, with the back facing up so that the piping stitches will be your guide, and stitch over them all around 3 sides and 4 corners of the pillow.

**4.** Trim seam allowance and clip corners. Turn right-side-out and press.

**5.** Stuff the pillow firmly with a combination of stuffing and pine needles. The stuffing will cushion the pine needles so they won't stick through the fabric. Slip-stitch the opening closed.

## GINGERBREAD MAN TOWEL TRIMS

You can dress up red-checked kitchen towels for the holidays for yourself or as gifts, using an easy-to-stitch gingerbread man appliqué. Children love to help with this project, which they can then give to a teacher or favorite adult. It will take about an hour from start to finish.

### Materials

red-checked linen kitchen towel

small amount of brown calico fabric

½ yard red embroidery floss

4 small white buttons

tracing paper

white glue

### Directions

*Note:* If you don't have a zigzag attachment on your sewing machine, cut each appliqué piece ¼ inch larger than the pattern size all around. (See page 15 for hand-appliqué details.)

**1.** Trace the gingerbread man pattern and pin it to the brown calico fabric. Cut out 2, or as many as needed if you wish to place them completely across the towel from one side to the other.

**2.** Mark the center of the bottom edge of the towel with a pin.

**3.** Pin each gingerbread cutout on either side of the center pin, about 1 inch from the bottom edge of the towel.

**4.** Using a zigzag stitch and brown thread, stitch around edges of each appliqué.

**5.** Next, stitch 2 buttons in a row on the front of each gingerbread man, as shown in the photograph.

**6.** Tie a small red-floss bow and glue to the neck of each gingerbread man.

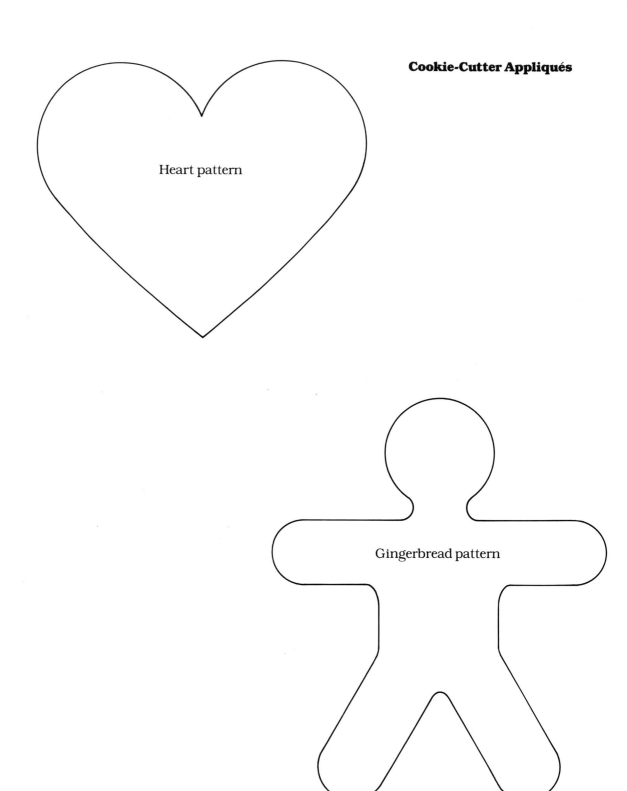

Heart pattern

Gingerbread pattern

# Patchwork Heart Pillow

Red-and-white triangles make up a patchwork of red-and-white squares that can be cut into any shape. This has always been a popular pattern and color scheme with quiltmakers. It is bold and graphic, and, when used to make a heart pillow, makes a definite statement. This is a country accessory that looks good almost anywhere you place it. It's an easy quilting project and one that you can pick up as lapwork whenever you have a few extra minutes.

The finished pillow measures 14 inches high and 18 inches across; it was made by my daughter, Robby Smith.

## Materials

*Note:* Yardages are figured for fabric 45 inches wide.

¼ yard white fabric

½ yard red fabric

2 yards 2-inch-wide pregathered eyelet ruffle

10 × 14-inch piece of thin batting

stuffing

tracing paper

## Directions

*Note:* The following directions are for the quick-and-easy right-triangle method. (See page 18.)

**1.** Enlarge the heart pattern (see page 35) and cut out.

**2.** Pin the pattern to the red fabric in such a way as to have enough fabric left over to complete step 3. Cut around outline for the backing.

**3.** Measure and mark 27 squares, each 3 × 3 inches, on the wrong side of the red fabric (3 rows of 9 squares each).

**4.** Draw a diagonal line through all squares.

**5.** With right sides facing, pin the red fabric to the same-size piece of white fabric.

**6.** Stitch ¼ inch on each side of all diagonal lines, through both thicknesses.

**7.** Cut on all solid lines. Open seams and press. You will have 54 squares made from red-and-white triangles.

*To make rows*

**1.** With right sides facing and raw edges aligned, stitch 2 squares together along one edge. Colors should be in same position, red at right, white at left. Open seams and press.

**2.** Continue to join squares in this way to make a horizontal row of 5 squares. The red part of each square should always be on the right. (See Figure 1.) Open seams and press.

**3.** Make 3 rows of 5 squares each.

**4.** Make 4 rows of 8 squares each.

**5.** Make 1 row of 7 squares.

*To join rows*

**1.** With right sides facing and long, raw edges aligned, pin a row of 5 squares to another row of 5 squares, being sure that square seams line up. Stitch. Open seams and press. Squares will line up across and down.

**2.** Continue in this way with another row of 5 squares, followed by 4 rows of 8 squares and ending with the row of 7 squares, as shown in Figure 2. Open seams and press.

**3.** Place the heart pattern on the patchwork fabric on an angle, as shown in Figure 3. Pin. Cut around outline.

**34**

### To quilt

**1.** Pin patchwork heart on the thin batting and cut around.
**2.** Remove top piece and trim batting ¼ inch all around.
**3.** Repin the top piece to the trimmed batting around the edges and in the center to secure.
**4.** Using white thread on the white triangles and red on the red triangles, quilt along all seam lines with a small running stitch. (See page 16 for quilting details.) Stitch only to batting edge, not into ¼-inch seam allowance of top fabric.

### To finish

**1.** With right sides facing and raw edges aligned, stitch short ends of eyelet ruffle together. With raw edges aligned, pin the eyelet ruffle around the edge of the pillow top.
**2.** Using white thread, stitch all around.
**3.** With right sides facing and raw edges aligned, stitch the backing to the pillow top, with the ruffle between, leaving a small opening in one side for turning. Turn right-side-out and press.
**4.** Stuff pillow firmly and slip-stitch opening closed.

**Patchwork Heart Pillow**

Figure 1. To make a row

Figure 2. To join rows

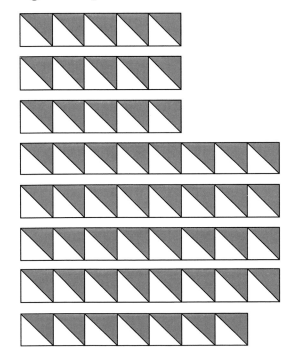

Figure 3. Heart pattern

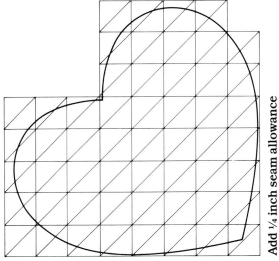

Add ¼ inch seam allowance

Each square equals 1 inch

# Year-Round Wreath

If you have an old quilt that is too far gone to repair, there are marvelous uses for it. The Amish, known for their exquisite quilts, also make wonderful small items with the remnants of old patchwork. The tiniest scraps can be put to use for dollmaking, garlands of hearts for hanging all year long, and sachets. This country wreath is decorated with a patchwork bear and hearts made from worn-out quilt material. The directions tell you how to reproduce the look with new, faded material—such as denim, muslin, and kitchen towels—if you don't have an old piece of quilt. Blue and white is one of the most popular traditional color schemes.

## Materials

8-inch round twig wreath (available in garden shops)
scraps of muslin, pale blue, and blue checked material
12 inches of ¼-inch-wide blue satin ribbon
stuffing
tracing paper

## Directions

*Note:* When cutting, add ¼-inch seam allowance around all pieces.
**1.** Trace the bear pattern and the heart pattern (see page 38) and cut out.
**2.** Pin the bear pattern to a piece of 4 × 5-inch muslin. Cut out for the backing. Pin the heart to a small piece of muslin. Cut 3.
**3.** If you are using a damaged quilt, cut another bear from a salvageable part. If not, cut the paper patterns apart on all lines and use these pieces to cut scraps of different blue-and-white fabrics with ¼-inch seam allowances.
**4.** To recreate the look, refer to the photograph. Arrange the patchwork pieces for the bear top. With right sides facing and straight edges aligned, stitch all pieces together. Press.
**5.** Repeat for hearts.
**6.** With right sides facing and raw edges aligned, stitch the backing and patchwork top pieces together, leaving a small opening on one side for turning.
**7.** Clip around all curves and turn right-side-out. Pack firmly with stuffing. Use a crochet hook or the eraser end of a pencil to push stuffing into bear's arms, legs, and ears. Do the same for the points and curves of the little hearts.
**8.** Turn raw edges of opening to inside and slip-stitch closed.
**9.** Tie the ribbon bow around the bear's neck.

## To finish

**1.** Arrange the hearts so they are evenly spaced around the bottom of the wreath and glue or stitch in place.

**2.** Set the bear in the center of the bottom portion of the wreath and stitch or glue in place.

**3.** Add sprigs of dried flowers to the wreath, if desired, and hang.

If you want to make more of these tiny patchwork hearts and bears, they can be stitched together to make a garland, a delightful country decoration. See page 95 in the Homespun Christmas section for a similar project done in red and green with larger hearts and gingerbread men.

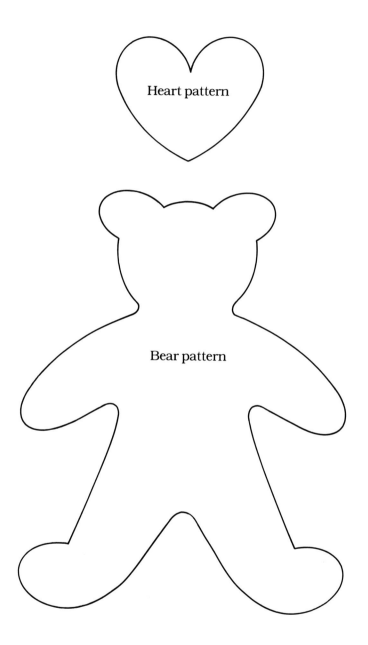

Heart pattern

Bear pattern

# American Beauty Sachets

After making a rose-chintz quilt, I had leftover pieces of fabric. Since it was an expensive print, I didn't want to throw any of it away. I decided that the beautiful rose colors, combined with blue ribbons and green leaves, would make elegant little sachets or pincushions. The flowers could be quilted around the outline and inside all details for an interesting project without any patchwork or appliqué. This is a nice, small quilting project that is worthy of gift-giving. Simply choose a floral print that is large enough to fill a 3- or 4-inch-square area. The rose-shaped sachets are about 2 inches square and cut to the shape of the flower, then quilted.

## Materials

floral fabric scraps, 3 to 4 inches square

solid fabric pieces in a color that matches the print

piping to go around a square or round sachet (1 package)

½ yard ¼-inch-wide satin ribbon, for rose-shaped sachets

thin batting

stuffing

potpourri

## Directions

**1.** Cut fabric square with ¼ inch extra fabric around the flower. This is your seam allowance. The flower should fill the entire area after stitching.

**2.** Cut a piece of solid fabric for the backing. Cut a piece of quilt batting ¼ inch smaller than the fabric.

**3.** Pin printed fabric to the batting and, with small, even stitches, quilt around the outline and all detail areas of the flower, leaves, and so on. (See page 16 for quilting details.)

**4.** With right sides facing and raw edges aligned, pin piping around top edge of the fabric. Stitch around, as close to cording as possible.

**5.** With right sides facing, pin backing to sachet top, with piping between. Turn work over, and, using the piping stitches as a guide, stitch around 3 sides and 4 corners, leaving small area open for turning.

**6.** Trim corners and turn right-side-out. Fill sachet with potpourri. Turn raw edges in and slip-stitch closed.

## ROSE-SHAPED SACHETS

**1.** Adding ¼ inch fabric all around, cut a flower shape from printed fabric.

**2.** Using this as your pattern guide, cut a solid piece for the backing.

**3.** With right sides facing and raw edges aligned, pin front and backing together and stitch around, leaving a small opening at the top for turning.

**4.** Clip around all curves and turn right-side-out. Press.

**5.** Fill with a small amount of stuffing. Push into all points and curves so that the sachet has puffiness but isn't too full. Add a drop of perfume to the stuffing.

**6.** Cut a 4-inch length of satin ribbon and fold in half lengthwise to make a loop. Overlap raw ends of the ribbon and insert into the opening at the top of the sachet. Pin in place.

**7.** Make a bow with the remaining ribbon and tack in place at the top of the sachet, catching the loop ends and closing the opening.

### To quilt

**1.** Thread your needle and make a small knot on the end of the thread. Insert needle from back to front in the center of the flower. Pull the knot through the backing so that it catches in the stuffing inside. Pull gently in order to make an indentation on the front of the sachet, to define the center of the flower and give it dimension.

**2.** Taking small, even stitches, quilt around all lines of the flower print. This will give it a sculptured look.

Hang in a closet or place in a lace-filled basket to put in the bathroom. I filled a basket with dried lavender and arranged the sachets with it. You might consider giving them as gifts alone, or with lingerie or guest towels.

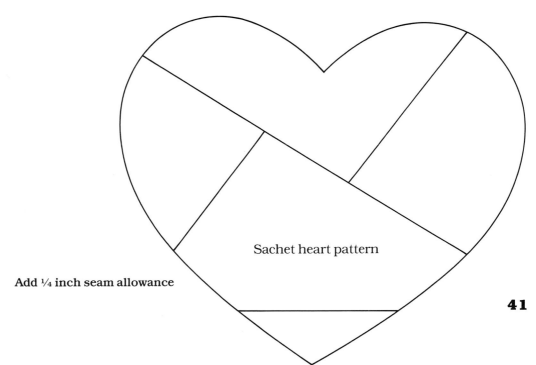

Add ¼ inch seam allowance

Sachet heart pattern

# Living With Country Style

**W**hat is country style? We hear about American country, French and Italian country, regional country, and all sorts of other kinds. Perhaps country style in America has always meant plain, unadorned, and functional. This is what our early settlers had in mind when they pieced together patches from worn clothing to make quilts, or gathered twigs for weaving into baskets. Born of necessity, most hand-crafted items were made without giving a thought to their artistic value.

How does country style fit into our way of living? In our hurried world of disposable, mass-produced items, it is comforting to own something that has been made by hand. It is reassuring that we can still take scraps of plain, ordinary cotton fabric and stitch them together to make an attractive wall hanging or pillow. These are the things that give us pleasure and add to the beauty of our homes.

Country accessories make a home warm and inviting. They make a statement that the people who live there care about their environment. The items themselves aren't unique, but it is their very simplicity that makes them so charming. We never seem to tire of them. Quilt patterns, for example, so often copied and reinterpreted, are confirmation that we want to add to and continue an American tradition.

The projects in this section, and in fact throughout the book, were designed to foster an interest in our most celebrated craft. Patchwork and quilting are as old as this country. By learning to make simple projects, you will be keeping this tradition alive. You can pass it on to future generations. Years from now, when our great-great-grandchildren are looking through our attics, they will count our quilting projects among their most prized family heirlooms.

# Classic American Pillows

Both of these pillows were made using the same star pattern. This is a good example of how you can make one pattern look different and create coordinated variations with one design. The same fabrics were used for both, but the pattern pieces were cut from different colors. The plaid is another version of homespun. Combined with the earth-tone colors, this is an interesting departure from the traditional calico. These 18-inch-square pillows would be quite handsome in a den or country living room.

## Pillow #1

### Materials

*Note:* Yardages are figured for all fabric 45 inches wide, except plaid homespun, which is 52 inches wide.

small piece red fabric (A)

⅛ yard light beige fabric (B)

¾ yard brown plaid homespun (C)

¼ yard tan fabric (D), *or* 1 yard 45-inch-wide fabric

2 yards cording

18-inch square of thin batting (if hand quilting is desired)

18-inch pillow form *or* stuffing

### Directions

*Note:* All measurements include ¼-inch seam allowance.

*Cut the following:*

from red (A):

    4 squares, each 2¾ × 2¾ inches

from light beige (B):

    4 squares, each 2¾ × 2¾ inches

    8 squares, each 3¼ × 3¼ inches. Cut each square into 2 triangles.

from brown plaid homespun (C):

    1 square, 5 × 5 inches

    4 squares, each 3¼ × 3¼ inches. Cut each square into 2 triangles.

    4 rectangles, each 2¾ × 14 inches

    1 square, 18½ × 18½ inches

from tan (D):

    4 rectangles, each 2¾ × 5 inches

    4 squares, each 2¾ × 2¾ inches

    4 squares, each 3¼ × 3¼ inches. Cut each square into 2 triangles.

**1.** With right sides facing and raw edges aligned, stitch a C triangle to a B triangle along the diagonal to make a square, as shown in Figure 1. Open seams and press. Make 8.

**2.** Next, stitch remaining *B* triangles to *D* triangles to make 8 squares. Open seams and press.

*To make a row*

**1.** With right sides facing and raw edges aligned, stitch a *B* square to a *C/B* square, as shown in Figure 2. Open seams and press.

**2.** Continue to join squares in the sequence shown in Figure 2 to make a row.

**3.** Continue to join squares and rectangles in rows, as shown in Figure 2. Open seams and press.

### To join rows

**1.** With right sides facing and raw edges aligned, stitch row 1 to row 2 along the long edge.

**2.** Continue to join rows in this way to make the block.

### To join borders

**1.** With right sides facing and raw edges aligned, stitch a *C* strip (2¾ × 14 inches) to each side of the pieced block along the long edges. Open seams and press. (See Figure 3.)

**2.** Next, stitch a *D* square to each short end of the remaining 2 *C* strips. Open seams and press.

**3.** With right sides facing and raw edges aligned, stitch these strips to the top and bottom edges of the pillow block, as shown in Figure 3.

### To quilt

These pillows are quite handsome when pieced and left as a simple patchwork project. If you'd like to add the dimension of hand-quilting, however, do the following:

**1.** Pin the patchwork-pillow top to the thin batting and baste in position with long stitches.

**2.** Using matching thread, take small running stitches ¼ inch in on each side of all seam lines. (See page 16 for quilting details.)

### To finish

**1.** Cut and piece strips of brown plaid or red fabric to make a long strip (1½ × 72½ inches) for the piping.

**2.** Beginning ½ inch from the end of the fabric, encase the cording in the fabric, and, using a zipper foot, stitch as close to cording as possible.

**3.** With right sides facing and raw edges aligned, pin the piping around the edge of the pillow top. Turn raw ends of piping fabric strip to inside and lap folded edge over covered cording. Pin in place. Stitch around, as close to cording as possible.

**4.** With right sides facing and raw edges aligned, using the piping stitches as a guide, stitch the backing piece to the pillow top around 3 sides and 4 corners.

**5.** Clip corners and turn right-side-out. Press.

**6.** Insert pillow form or stuff. Turn raw edges to the inside and slip-stitch opening closed.

## PILLOW #2

Use the same design and alternate the colors to create matching pillows.

**Classic American Pillows**

Figure 1

Figure 2

Row 1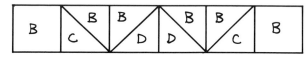

Row 2

Row 3

Row 4

Row 5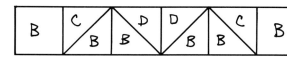

Figure 3

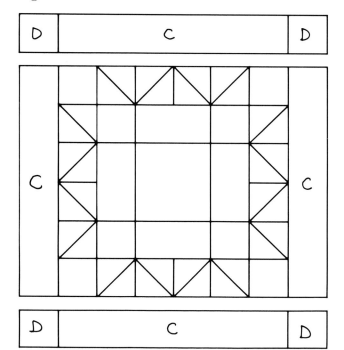

**46**

# Rose Place Mats

Make a set of patchwork place mats with matching napkins in our blue-and-white rose print combined with solid blue trim. One of the things I like about making my own place mats is that I can customize them to go with my room and china. I can also make the mats and napkins for a fraction of what it would cost to buy them, and it's an easy sewing project. A set of 4 makes a very nice wedding, shower, or housewarming gift. Consider making chair-seat covers as well. You could use the patchwork patterns for our stool seats on page 59 with the place mat fabric. These place mats are 14 × 18 inches. Directions are given for making 4.

## Materials

*Note:* Yardages are figured for fabric 45 inches wide.

½ yard printed fabric (*A*)

½ yard blue fabric (*B*)

1 yard backing fabric

thin batting

## PLACE MATS

### Directions

*Note:* All measurements include ¼-inch seam allowance.

*Cut the following:*

from rose print (*A*):    4 rectangles, each 10½ × 14½ inches
                         16 squares, each 2½ × 2½ inches

from blue (*B*):    8 rectangles, each 2½ × 10½ inches
                  8 rectangles, each 2½ × 14½ inches

**1.** With right sides facing and raw edges aligned, stitch a short blue (*B*) rectangle to each side edge of a rose (*A*) rectangle, as shown in Figure 1. Open seams and press.

**2.** Next, stitch a rose (*A*) square to each short edge of a long blue (*B*) rectangle to make a longer strip, as shown in Figure 2. Open seams and press. Make 2 strips.

**3.** With right sides facing and raw edges aligned, join these strips to the top and bottom edges of the rose rectangle, as shown in Figure 2. Open seams and press. This is the patchwork front of the place mat. Make 4.

*To quilt*

**1.** Cut a piece of quilt batting ¼ inch smaller than the place mat top all around.

**2.** Cut the backing piece, 14½ × 18½ inches. With wrong sides facing and batting between, pin the top and backing together.

**3.** For a quick project, machine-stitch along each seam line, ending ¼ inch before reaching outer edges all around. If you want to hand-quilt, take small running stitches ¼ inch in from each seam line through all 3 layers of material. Do not stitch into the outside edge seam allowance. (See page 16 for quilting details.)

*To finish*

**1.** Turn raw edges of the top piece under ¼ inch and press.

**2.** Turn backing edges to the inside ¼ inch and press.

**3.** Slip-stitch closed and then machine-stitch all around as close to outside edge as possible.

## NAPKINS

*Note:* I used the rose print for each napkin. Sometimes it's fun to mix prints and solids so you have 2 of each, or even different prints in the same color. Our napkins are 18 inches square when finished. If you make them slightly smaller, you can get 2 napkins out of ½ yard of fabric. Turn the edges under slightly, press, then turn again and machine-stitch all around. If you want to make larger napkins, cut each one 18 inches square and add a 1-inch to 2-inch border of solid blue fabric all around.

### Rose Place Mats

Figure 1

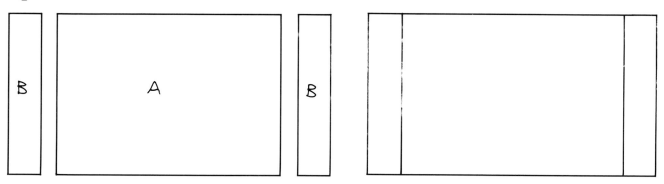

Figure 2

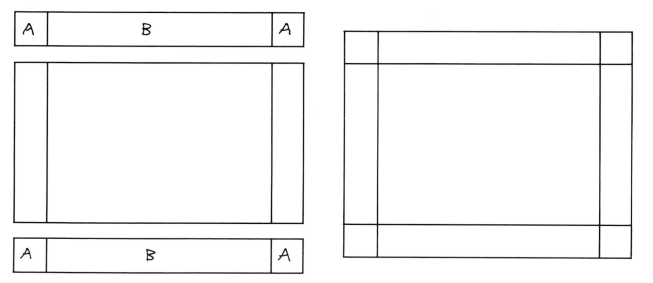

# Appliqué Accent Pillows

Country pillows add warmth and charm to any area of the house. These are smaller in size than decorative pillows normally used for backrests or to go on sofas and chairs. They are meant as accents to place in front of another pillow or in the crook of the arm of a chair. They are made mostly with calico fabrics, so popular in quilting and country projects. The simple appliqués can be applied by hand or with a zigzag stitch on the machine. See page 15 for appliqué details. Because they are relatively small, these pillows are inexpensive to make; they are good bazaar items, gifts, or home accessories.

## WATERMELON PILLOW

The finished size is 8 × 10 inches.

### Materials

*Note:* Yardages are figured for fabric 45 inches wide.

black fabric scraps

small piece red fabric

small piece green fabric

¼ yard white-and-red calico print, predominantly white

1 yard green piping

stuffing

tracing paper

cardboard for template

chalk

### Directions

**1.** Trace each part of the watermelon design and cut out.

**2.** Pin the rind pattern to the green fabric and cut one piece. Pin the watermelon wedge to the red fabric and cut one.

**3.** Use the seed pattern to make a cardboard template. (See page 14.) Use this template and a piece of chalk to draw 15 seeds on the black fabric. Cut out all pieces.

**4.** Cut 2 pieces of white-and-red calico, each 8½ × 10½ inches, for the top and back of the pillow.

**5.** Pin the watermelon appliqué pieces in position on the center top of one piece of fabric.

**6.** Using a zigzag stitch and matching thread, stitch around the edges of each appliqué piece. I used green around the outside edge of the rind, as well as the inside edge where the red and green fabrics meet. Use red thread across the top part of the watermelon slice, and green across the top of the rind on each side.

*To finish*

**1.** With right sides facing and raw edges aligned, pin the piping around the edge of the pillow top, overlapping the raw ends.

**2.** Stitch around, as close to cording as possible.

**3.** With right sides facing, pin the backing piece to the top piece with the piping between. Be sure all raw edges of the back, piping, and top are even.

**4.** With the back facing up, using the piping stitches as a guide, stitch over them all around 3 sides and 4 corners of the pillow.

**5.** Trim seam allowance and clip corners. Turn right-side-out and press.

**6.** Stuff the pillow and turn the raw edges to the inside. Slip-stitch opening closed.

## APPLE APPLIQUE PILLOW

The finished size is $10 \times 10$ inches, with a 2-inch ruffle.

### Materials

green calico scraps

⅓ yard red calico

⅓ yard white calico

1¼ yards red piping

stuffing

tracing paper

### Directions

**1.** Trace apple, leaves, and stems separately. Cut out.

**2.** Pin the apple pattern to red calico. Pin the stem and leaves to green calico. Cut out each piece.

**3.** Cut 2 squares, each 10½ × 10½ inches, from the white calico for the top and back of the pillow.

**4.** Pin the apple, stem, and leaves in the center of the top piece of white calico.

**5.** Use a zigzag stitch and matching thread to stitch around each raw edge.

*To finish*

**1.** With right sides facing and raw edges aligned, pin the piping all around the edge of the pillow top, overlapping the ends. Stitch around, as close to cording as possible.

**2.** Cut and piece 2 strips of red calico together to make one long strip, 2¾ × 80 inches, for the ruffle.

**3.** With right sides facing and short ends together, join the red calico strip.

**4.** Turn one long edge under ¼ inch and press. Turn another ¼ inch under, press, and stitch all around.

**5.** Divide ruffle into 4 equal parts. Mark with pins.

**6.** With right sides facing and raw edges aligned, pin the ruffle strip to the pillow top, gathering the fabric between pin markings to fit each side.

**7.** Using the piping stitches as a guide, stitch all around.

**8.** With right sides facing and raw edges aligned, pin the backing piece to the pillow top with the ruffle and piping between. Stitch around 3 sides and 4 corners.

**9.** Trim seam allowance and clip corners. Turn right-side-out and press.

**10.** Stuff pillow firmly. Fold raw edges to inside and slip-stitch opening closed.

**52**

## FARM SCENE PILLOW

The finished size is 10 × 13 inches, with a 2-inch ruffle.

### Materials

fabric scraps: brown, black, and a white textured fabric, such as dotted swiss, for the lamb.

dark-green calico strip, 2½ × 13½ inches

⅓ yard light-blue fabric for pillow top and backing

¼ yard rose fabric

1½ yards brown piping

stuffing

tracing paper

### Directions

**1.** Trace each part of each farm-animal shape separately. Cut out each piece.

**2.** Pin the cow pattern to brown fabric, the spots to white fabric, the rooster to rose fabric, the lamb to white fabric, and the lamb's nose and legs to black fabric. Cut out all pieces and set aside.

**3.** Cut one piece of light-blue fabric, 8½ × 13½ inches.

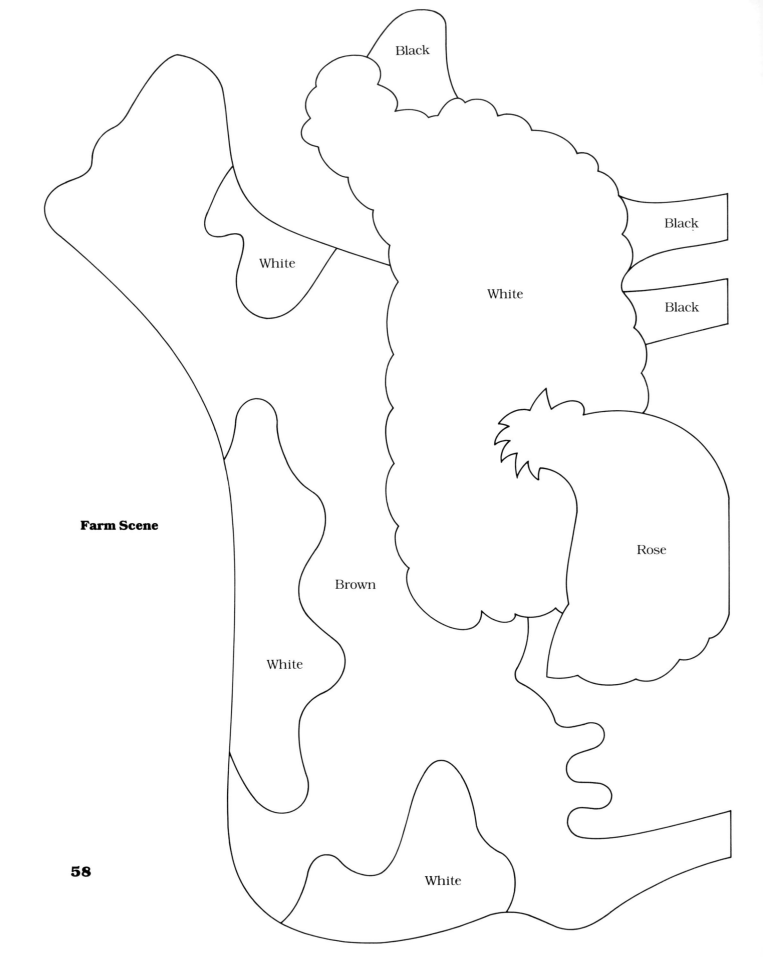

Black

Black

Black

White

White

Rose

Brown

White

White

**Farm Scene**

**58**

# FARM SCENE PILLOW

The finished size is $10 \times 13$ inches, with a 2-inch ruffle.

## Materials

fabric scraps: brown, black, and a white textured fabric, such as dotted swiss, for the lamb.

dark-green calico strip, $2\frac{1}{2} \times 13\frac{1}{2}$ inches

$\frac{1}{3}$ yard light-blue fabric for pillow top and backing

$\frac{1}{4}$ yard rose fabric

$1\frac{1}{2}$ yards brown piping

stuffing

tracing paper

## Directions

**1.** Trace each part of each farm-animal shape separately. Cut out each piece.

**2.** Pin the cow pattern to brown fabric, the spots to white fabric, the rooster to rose fabric, the lamb to white fabric, and the lamb's nose and legs to black fabric. Cut out all pieces and set aside.

**3.** Cut one piece of light-blue fabric, $8\frac{1}{2} \times 13\frac{1}{2}$ inches.

**4.** With right sides facing and raw edges aligned, join the green calico strip to the bottom of the blue fabric piece to make the pillow top. Open seams and press.

**5.** Pin the animal pieces in position on the fabric. Using a zigzag stitch and matching thread, stitch around edges of each appliqué piece.

*To finish*

**1.** Stitch brown piping around top of pillow, as directed for the Apple Appliqué Pillow.

**2.** Cut a piece of rose fabric to make one long strip, 2¾ × 92 inches, for the ruffle. Make and join ruffle to pillow top as for the Apple Appliqué Pillow.

**3.** Cut backing piece, 8½ × 13½ inches, from light-blue fabric.

**4.** Join back to top as for the Apple Appliqué Pillow, and finish in the same way.

## BASKET OF FRUIT APPLIQUE PILLOW

The finished size is 10 × 10 inches, with a 2-inch ruffle.

### Materials

fabric scraps: red, yellow, green
white calico square, 10½ × 10½ inches
⅓ yard blue calico
1¼ yards blue piping
stuffing
tracing paper

### Directions

**1.** Trace each shape for the fruit and basket. Cut out each piece.

**2.** Pin the apple parts to red fabric and the pear to yellow fabric. Cut each one out. Pin the stems to green fabric and cut out.

**3.** Pin the basket and handle to blue calico and cut out.

**4.** Pin each fabric piece to the 10½-inch square of white calico.

**5.** Using a zigzag stitch and matching thread, stitch around all edges to secure the appliqués.

*To finish*

**1.** Pin piping to front of pillow top and stitch around as for the Farm Scene Pillow.

**2.** Cut and piece blue calico to make one long strip, 2¾ × 80 inches, for the ruffle. Make and join ruffle to pillow top as for Farm Scene Pillow.

**3.** Cut backing piece, 10½ × 10½ inches, from blue calico.

**4.** Join back to top as for the Farm Scene Pillow, and finish in the same way.

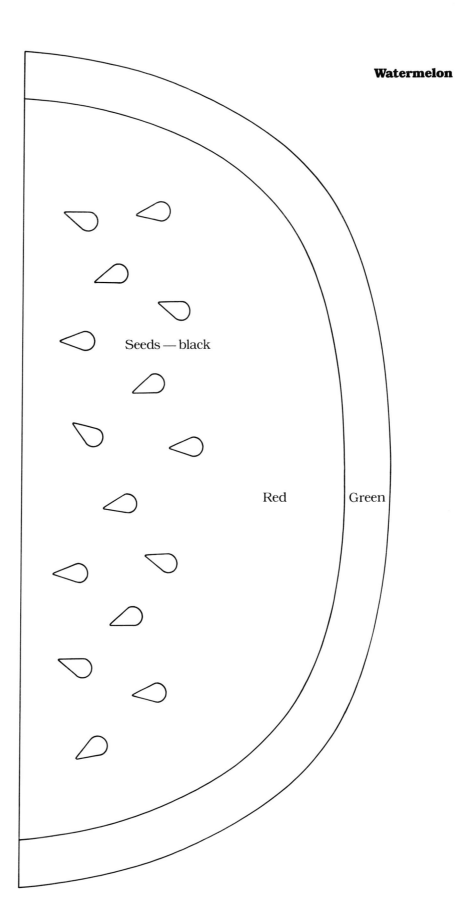

**Watermelon**

Seeds — black

Red          Green

**55**

# Apple

**Basket of Fruit**

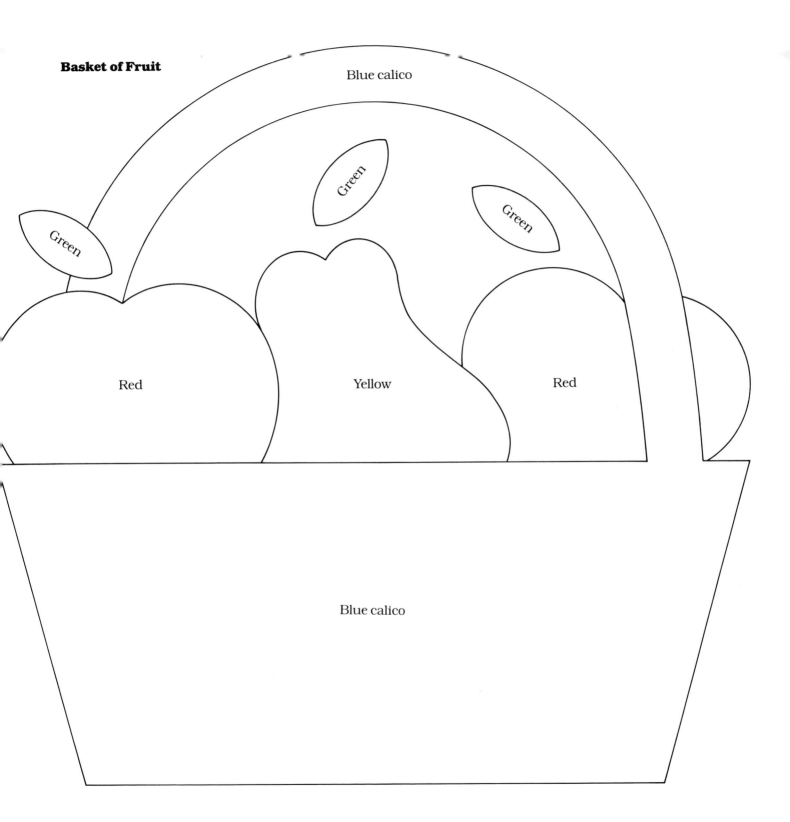

Blue calico

Green

Green

Green

Green

Red

Yellow

Red

Blue calico

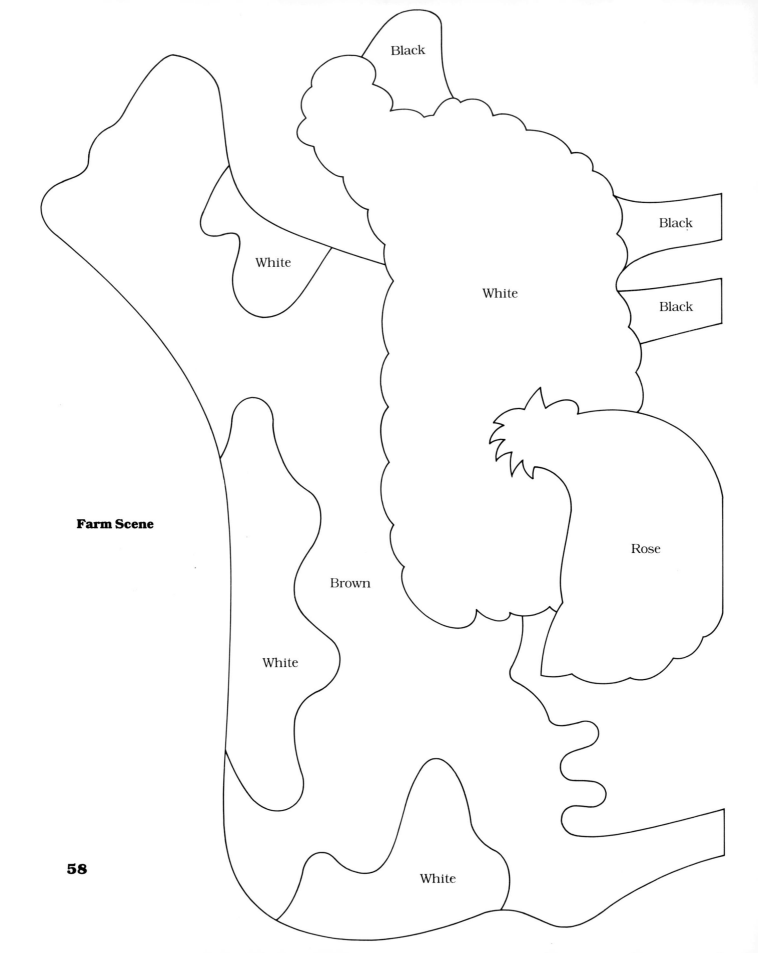

Black

White

Black

Black

White

**Farm Scene**

Brown

White

Rose

White

58

# Sitting Pretty Seat Covers

Last year, I sent my mother a box of fabric left over from various projects I had made. She always knows how to turn remnants into something worthwhile, and, sure enough, she designed these stool covers in pretty patchwork designs. One is a star; the other is the popular bow-tie pattern. This is a wonderful way to use up small pieces of fabric, and the hand-quilting gives each one a special quality. I think they're interesting because they don't match. Consider making different, rather than matching, seat covers for stools or dining-room chairs. These seat covers measure 17 inches in diameter.

## STAR PATTERN SEAT COVER

### Materials

*Note:* Yardages are figured for fabric 45 inches wide.

¼ yard wine-colored calico (*A*)

½ yard white *or* muslin fabric (*B*)

1½ yards piping

tracing paper

cardboard for template

thin batting

### Directions

**1.** Trace the pattern piece and transfer it to the cardboard for a template. (See page 14.) Cut out.

**2.** Place the template on the wrong side of the wine calico and trace around it 32 times. Repeat on the white or muslin 16 times. Cut out all pieces.

**3.** With right sides facing and raw edges aligned, stitch a wine (*A*) piece to a white (*B*) piece, followed by another wine (*A*) piece, as shown in Figure 1. Open seams and press.

**4.** With right sides facing and raw edges aligned, join another *A* piece to another *B* piece. Open seams and press.

**5.** With right sides facing and raw edges aligned, stitch the strip with 3 pieces to the strip with 2 pieces, adding an *A* piece to the bottom edge, as shown in Figure 2. This represents ⅛ of the star shape. Make 8 pieces in this way.

**6.** With right sides facing and raw edges aligned, stitch 4 of the pointed pieces together to make half of the star. (See Figure 3.) Open seams and press. Repeat with the other 4 pointed pieces.

**7.** With right sides facing and raw edges aligned, stitch both halves together. Open seams and press. (See Figure 4.)

## To appliqué

**1.** Cut 2 circles, each 18 inches in diameter, from the white fabric. One piece is the top, the other is the backing.
**2.** Position the star in the center of one white circle. Turn all edges of the star under ¼ inch all around, press and pin to the top fabric.
**3.** Using tiny slip-stitches, appliqué the star to the seat top. (See page 15 for hand-appliqué details.) Remove pins.

## To make ties and piping

**1.** Cut a piece of wine-colored fabric, 2 × 18½ inches, for each seat tie needed (4 for stools, 2 for chair backs).
**2.** Turn raw edges under ¼ inch and press. Fold the strip in half lengthwise and press. Stitch across ends and along the open long edge.

## To finish

**1.** With right sides facing and raw edges aligned, pin the piping around the top of the stool cover. Fold each tie in half, and pin the folded end in place over the piping. (The loose ends of the tie will be toward the center of the cover for now.)
**2.** With right sides facing and raw edges aligned, pin the backing circle to the top piece and then to the batting.
**3.** Stitch around, with the piping and tie strips between, leaving a few inches open for turning.
**4.** Clip around into the seam allowance. Turn right-side-out. Turn raw edges under, press, and slip-stitch closed.

## To quilt

**1.** Pin all 3 layers together.
**2.** Take small running stitches, through all 3 layers, ¼ inch in on both sides of all appliqué star seams. (See page 16 for quilting details.)

Detail: Bow-Tie Seat Cover

# BOW-TIE SEAT COVER

## Materials

*Note:* Yardages are figured for fabric 45 inches wide.

light solid and calico scraps

small piece of dark gray solid or calico (*A*)

small piece of red solid or calico (*B*)

small piece of light gray solid or calico (*C*)

½ yard white fabric

2 yards red piping

tracing paper

cardboard for templates

thin batting

## Directions

### To make bow-tie block

**1.** Trace the pattern pieces and transfer to cardboard for the templates. (See page 14.) Cut out.

**2.** Place Template 1 on *A* fabric and trace around the outline 6 times. Repeat on the *B* fabric 6 times, on *C* 6 times, and on the scraps of light solids and calicos 18 times.

**3.** Place Template 2 on the *A* fabric and trace around the outline 3 times, *B* 3 times, and *C* 3 times. Cut out all pieces.

**4.** Refer to Figure 1. With right sides facing and raw edges aligned, join 2 *A* pieces, 2 light pieces cut using Template 1 and 1 *A* piece cut using Template 2. Make 3. Open seams and press.

**5.** Repeat step 4, vary colors to make 3 blocks with *B* pieces and light pieces, and 3 blocks with *C* pieces and light pieces. Open seams and press.

### To join blocks (Refer to Figure 2)

**1.** With right sides facing and raw edges aligned, stitch an *A* block to a *B* block and then to a *C* block for row 1. Open seams and press.

**2.** Next, stitch a *C* block to an *A* block and then to a *B* block for row 2. Open seams and press.

**3.** To make row 3, join a *B* block to a *C* block and then to an *A* block. Open seams and press.

### To join rows

**1.** With right sides facing and raw edges aligned, join row 1 to row 2 and then to row 3 along the long edge.

**2.** Open seams and press.

### To finish

**1.** Cut 1 white circle, 18 inches in diameter.

**2.** Pin the bow-tie square to the circle. (The corners will extend beyond the circle.) Turn the edge of the square under ¼ inch and slip-stitch to the circle fabric.

**3.** Cut the backing piece to match the top piece.

**4.** With right sides facing and raw edges aligned, pin the piping around the edge of the patchwork top. Stitch around, as close to cording as possible.

**5.** Make the ties as for the Star Pattern Seat Cover, and finish in the same way.

**6.** To quilt, take small running stitches, through all 3 layers, ¼ inch in on both sides of all seams. (See page 16 for quilting details.)

## Star Pattern Seat Cover

### Figure 1

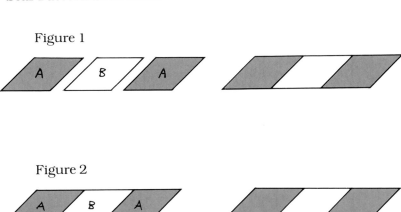

### Figure 2

### Figure 4

### Figure 3

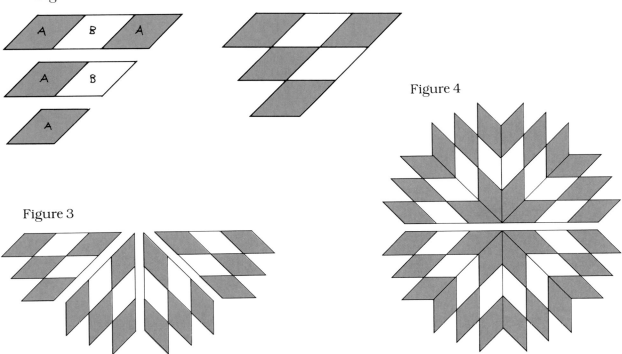

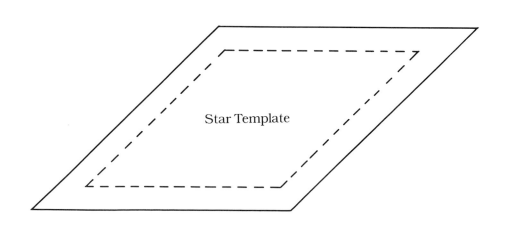

Star Template

## Bow-Tie Seat Cover

Figure 1. To make a block

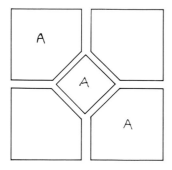

Figure 2. To join blocks

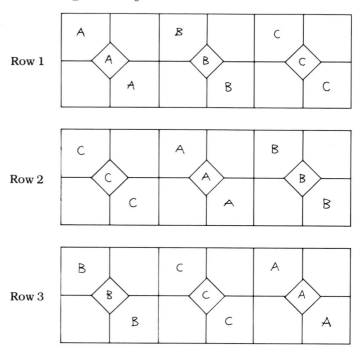

Row 1

Row 2

Row 3

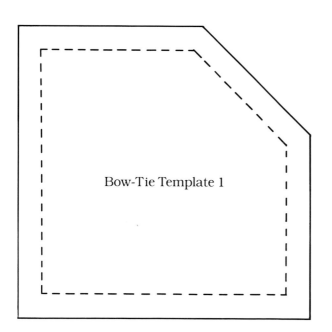

Bow-Tie Template 1

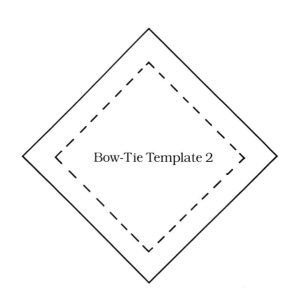

Bow-Tie Template 2

# Schoolhouse Wall Hanging

This classic design has been interpreted in many ways. Most often, it's been made in a series of blocks with lattice strips between to create a full-size quilt. In a departure from tradition, Susan Fernald Joyce and Margaret Detmer used the pattern to create a wall hanging without lattice strips. They think it would be nice as a hanging banner for the holidays. The finished size is 34 × 34 inches.

## Materials

*Note:* Yardages are figured for fabric 45 inches wide.

¾ yard red calico (you can use all one pattern or a combination)

1 yard solid white fabric

1 yard solid red fabric for backing

thin batting

tracing paper

cardboard for templates

## Directions

Trace all pattern pieces and transfer to cardboard to make templates. (See page 14 for template details.)

*Cut the following:*

*Note:* All measurements include ¼-inch seam allowance.

from red calico:

    borders: *No Black*

        2 strips, each 1¾ × 34½ inches, for sides

        2 strips, each 1¾ × 32 inches, for top and bottom

    (B) 8 rectangles, each 1½ × 2¾ inches

    (E) 4 rectangles, each 1½ × 7 inches

    (F) 12 rectangles, each 1½ × 5 inches

    (I) 8 rectangles, each 1¾ × 7 inches

    4 shapes from Template 2

    4 shapes from Template 4

from white:

    borders:

        2 strips, each 3 × 32 inches, for sides

        2 strips, each 3 × 27 inches, for top and bottom

    1 lattice strip, 3 × 27 inches

    2 lattice strips, each 3 × 12½ inches

    (A) 8 rectangles, each 1½ × 2⅝ inches

(C) 4 rectangles, each $1\frac{1}{2} \times 3\frac{3}{4}$ inches

(D) 4 rectangles, each $1\frac{1}{2} \times 7$ inches

(G) 8 rectangles, each $2\frac{1}{4} \times 5$ inches

(H) 4 rectangles, each $1\frac{3}{4} \times 7$ inches

(J) 4 rectangles, each $2\frac{1}{4} \times 7$ inches

(K) 4 strips, each $1\frac{1}{2} \times 12\frac{1}{2}$ inches

8 shapes from Template 1

4 shapes from Template 3

*Top half of block* (Refer to Figure 1)

**1.** With right sides facing and raw edges aligned, stitch a Template 1 piece to a Template 2 piece along the slanted edges, as shown in Figure 1a. Open seams and press.

**2.** Continue by joining pieces cut from Templates 3 and 4, and then another cut from Template 1, as shown in Figure 1a, to make a large rectangle. Open seams and press.

**3.** With right sides facing and raw edges aligned, stitch piece A to piece B along short edge. Open seams and press.

**4.** Continue by joining piece C, then another piece B, and ending with another piece A to make one long strip. Open seams and press. (See Figure 1b.)

**5.** With right sides facing and raw edges aligned, join the pieced strip to the top edge of the large pieced rectangle to make the top half of the block, as shown in Figure 1b.

*Bottom half of block* (Refer to Figure 2)

**1.** With right sides facing and raw edges aligned, stitch piece D to piece E along the long edge, as shown in Figure 2a. Open seams and press.

**2.** Next, join one F piece to each side of a G piece. Then add another G piece and finally a third F piece, as shown in Figure 2a. Open seams and press.

**3.** With right sides facing and raw edges aligned, stitch these 2 sections together. Open seams and press.

**4.** With right sides facing and raw edges aligned, stitch piece H to piece I along the edge. Next, join piece J and another piece I as shown in Figure 2b. Open seams and press.

**5.** With right sides facing and raw edges aligned, stitch Figure 2a section to Figure 2b section, as shown in Figure 2c. Open seams and press.

**6.** Next, stitch piece K to the bottom edge of the bottom half of the block. Open seams and press.

**7.** Refer to Figure 3. With right sides facing and raw edges aligned, stitch top half of the block to the bottom half of the block. Open seams and press. Make 4 blocks, 2 in reverse.

### To make a row
**1.** With right sides facing and raw edges aligned, stitch a block to a short white lattice piece along the long edge. Open seams and press.
**2.** Next, join another block (one made in reverse, as shown in Figure 4.) Open seams and press. Make 2 rows.

### To join rows
**1.** With right sides facing and raw edges aligned, join the bottom edge of a row to the top long edge of the long white lattice strip. Open seams and press.
**2.** Join the next row to make a square of 4 blocks, as shown in Figure 5.

### To join borders
**1.** With right sides facing, stitch short white borders to the top and bottom edges of the quilt top. Open seams and press.
**2.** Next, join the white side borders in the same way. Open seams and press.
**3.** With right sides facing, stitch shorter red border strips to the top and bottom edges of the quilt top. Open seams and press.
**4.** Join the red side border pieces in the same way.

### To quilt
**1.** Trace the quilting design and transfer it to the quilt top. (See page 16 for quilting details.)
**2.** Center the batting and quilt top on the wrong side of the backing so the extra fabric is even all around. Pin.
**3.** Beginning in the center and working outward in a sunburst pattern, baste the top, batting, and backing together, using long stitches through all 3 layers.
**4.** Using small running stitches, quilt along the lines of the quilt pattern.
**5.** When all quilting is complete, remove basting stitches.

### To finish
**1.** Turn the raw edges of the backing fabric forward ¼ inch and press all around.
**2.** Turn the extra fabric forward again over the edge of wall hanging top. Lap fabric at corners to make straight edge. Slip-stitch this border to top all around to finish.

### To hang
Attach a small piece of Velcro® to each corner and center of each side edge on the back of the wall hanging. Measuring carefully so your quilt will hang straight, attach corresponding pieces of Velcro® to the wall where your quilt will hang.

## Schoolhouse Wall Hanging

Figure 1. Top half of block

Figure 1a

Figure 2. Bottom half of block

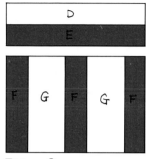

Figure 2a

Figure 2b

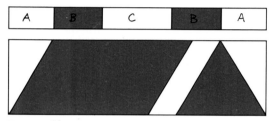

Figure 1b

Figure 3

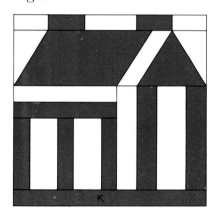

Figure 4. To make a row

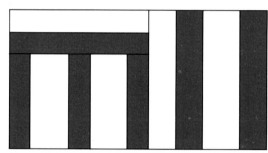

Figure 2c

Figure 5. To join rows

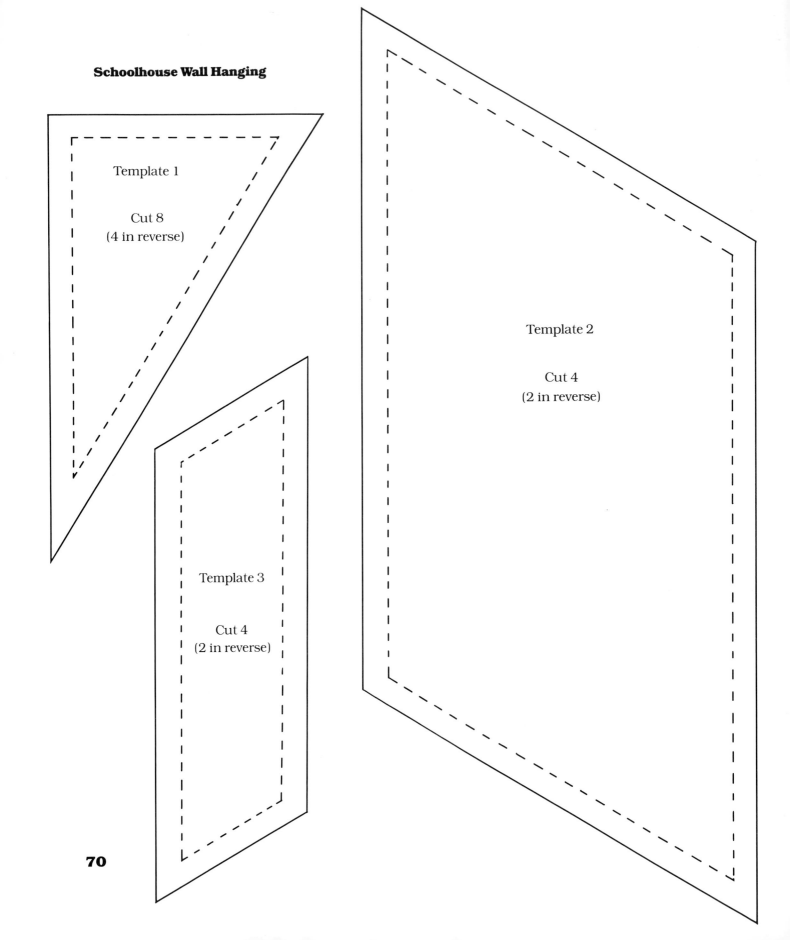

**Schoolhouse Wall Hanging**

Template 1

Cut 8
(4 in reverse)

Template 2

Cut 4
(2 in reverse)

Template 3

Cut 4
(2 in reverse)

**Schoolhouse Wall Hanging**

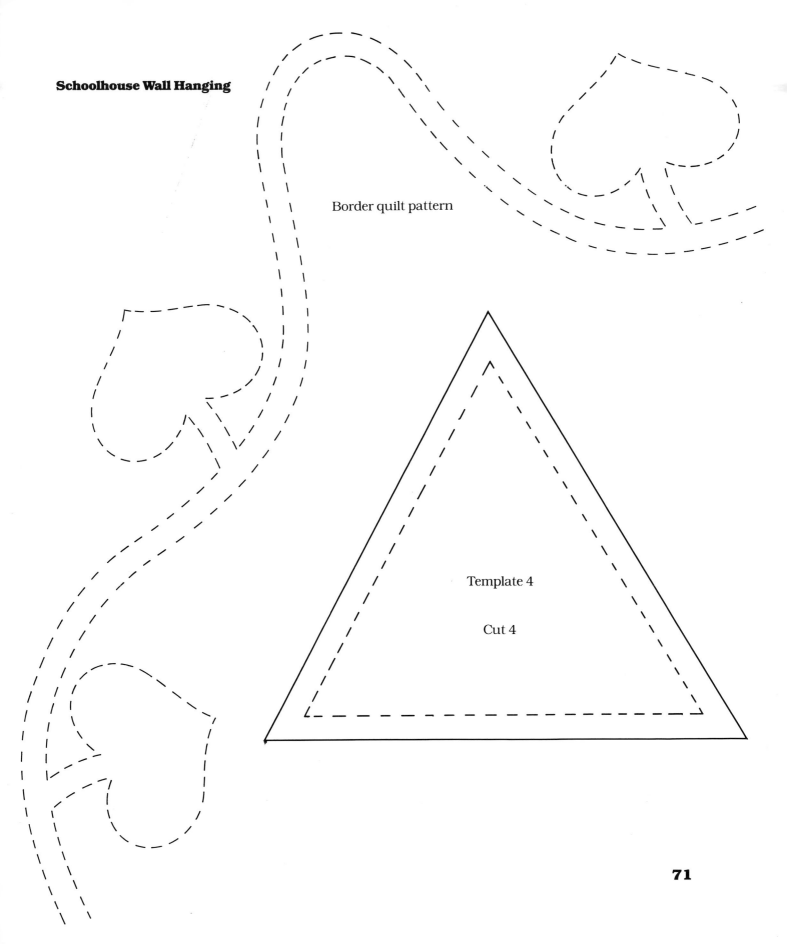

Border quilt pattern

Template 4

Cut 4

# Homespun Christmas

**H**omespun fabric is as traditional as country style. It is a fabric we're all familiar with, though we may not realize it. Homespun looks like woven fabric because it is the same on both front and back. There is no wrong side. It also has a woven quality because of its plaid or checked patterns, which come in country colors such as cranberry, sage, and blue on white or cream.

If you think about it, country rag dolls, place mats, pillows, and early-American-style clothing are all often made with homespun fabric. Homespun has substance. It is cotton fabric with the texture of linen, and is heavier than most cottons often used for the same projects. It has character, because it looks new and old at the same time. For all these reasons, it is the perfect fabric for crafting Christmas gifts and decorations that will last long after the tree has been taken down.

The projects in the following section show how homespun can be used over and over again for different projects and look appealing each time. I have used it for a full-length tablecloth, simple appliqués, ruffled pillows, Christmas stockings, and more. I never tire of it. In fact, these coordinated fabric accessories make my home warm and inviting during the holidays, without looking overly Christmaslike.

Choose one or make all of the projects. Some, like the potholder, can be made in less than an hour. Others, like the quilt, will take a weekend or more of your time. The smaller items make terrific gifts or bazaar items. You get a lot of mileage from homespun fabric, because it often comes 52 inches wide. You can find homespun at better fabric shops across the country; it comes in a wide variety of colors and in many different size checks and plaids.

# Holiday Touches

During the holidays, it's fun to dress up each room with touches of green and red, especially for Christmas. The homespun fabric used here comes in bright reds and greens as well as country cranberry and sage. For the kitchen, you might make a few potholders; for the dining area, heart-shaped place mats with matching appliquéd napkins; and—of course—an oversize stocking or two for the hearth.

## CHRISTMAS POTHOLDER

The finished size is 8 × 8 inches.

### Materials

small piece of green-checked homespun
small piece of red-checked homespun
batting, 16 × 16 inches
tracing paper

### Directions

*Note:* All measurements include ¼-inch seam allowance.

*Cut the following:*

from green check:

    1 square, 6½ × 6½ inches

from red check:

    1 square, 8½ × 8½ inches, for back
    2 strips, each 1½ × 6½ inches
    2 strips, each 1½ × 8½ inches
    1 strip, 1½ × 6 inches

Heart pattern

**1.** Trace the heart pattern and pin to a small piece of the red-checked fabric.

**2.** If appliqué will be attached with a machine zigzag stitch, cut the heart to the exact size of the pattern. If you want to hand-appliqué, add ¼ inch all around the fabric when cutting it out.

**3.** Pin the heart fabric to the center of the green square and stitch around edges with matching thread. If attaching appliqué by hand, see page 15 for details.

**4.** With right sides facing and raw edges aligned, stitch a 1½ × 6½-inch red strip to right and left side of the green square. Open seams and press.

**5.** Next, stitch the 1½ × 8½-inch red strips to the top and bottom of the green square. Open seams and press.

*To finish*

**1.** To make the hanging loop, fold the remaining red strip (1½ × 6 inches) in half lengthwise, with wrong sides facing. Turn the edges under ¼ inch and press. Stitch along the long edge.
**2.** Fold the loop in half with the raw ends overlapping and pin to one corner of the top with the loop toward the center of the potholder.
**3.** Cut the batting in half and pin one piece to the back of the patchwork top piece. Stitch together along all top seam lines.
**4.** Pin the second piece of batting to the wrong side of the back piece and stitch together ½ inch from edge.
**5.** With right sides facing, stitch top and backing together around 3 sides and 4 corners, catching loop ends in the stitching.
**6.** Clip corners and turn right-side-out. Fold raw edges to inside and slip-stitch opening closed.

## CHRISTMAS STOCKINGS

Homespun is a good fabric to use for Christmas stockings because it holds a shape. The checks and plaids in red and green can be combined, with one for the body and the other for the cuff. The patched heel and toe are made from a piece of solid-color felt. If you want to make a patchwork stocking, consider combining the 2 fabrics. The directions that follow are quite simple; you can easily make a row of matching stockings for all the children in the family. The stockings are 15 inches long; each square on the grid equals 1 inch.

### Materials (for 1 stocking)
¼ yard red plaid fabric
piece of green-checked fabric, 9 × 15 inches
piece of red felt, 9 × 12 inches
6 inches of ¾-inch-wide red or green satin ribbon
tracing paper

### Directions
**1.** Enlarge the stocking pattern and transfer to tracing paper. (See page 13.)
**2.** With wrong sides facing, fold the red fabric in half widthwise. Pin the stocking pattern on top of the fabric and cut out. You will have the front and back pieces of the stocking.
**3.** Enlarge the heel and toe patterns. (See page 13 for enlarging details.)
**4.** Pin the patterns to the red felt and cut 2 pieces for each.
**5.** Pin the heel and toe in position on the front and back pieces of the stockings, as indicated on the pattern pieces. Using red thread, stitch along only the straight edge of the heel and toe.

**6.** With right sides facing and raw edges aligned, pin the front and back of the stocking together. Beginning at one top edge and using a ¼-inch seam allowance, stitch around, leaving the top edge open. Trim seams and clip around curves. Turn right-side-out and press.

*To make cuff*

**1.** Enlarge and transfer cuff pattern to tracing paper. (See page 13.)

**2.** Use this pattern to cut 4 pieces of fabric for outside and lining of cuff.

**3.** With right sides together and raw edges aligned, stitch 2 cuff pieces together along the short ends. Repeat with the remaining 2 cuff pieces. Open seams and press, but do not turn to right side.

**4.** Slip one cuff over the other, right sides facing, and align seams and top raw edges. Pin around top and bottom edges.

**5.** Stitch around bottom (wider) edge only. Trim seam. Turn right-side-out and press.

*To finish*

**1.** Fold ribbon in half lengthwise to make a loop and overlap raw ends. With raw edges aligned at top edge and loop inside stocking, pin at top of side seam.

**2.** Slip the entire cuff inside the stocking and pin around top raw edge. Loop will be between stocking and cuff.

**3.** Stitch around, leaving a ¼-inch seam allowance.

**4.** Trim seam and turn the cuff right-side-out over the top of the stocking. Pull loop up and stitch around the outside top edge of the cuff for a neat finish.

**Each square equals 1 inch**

**Christmas Stocking**

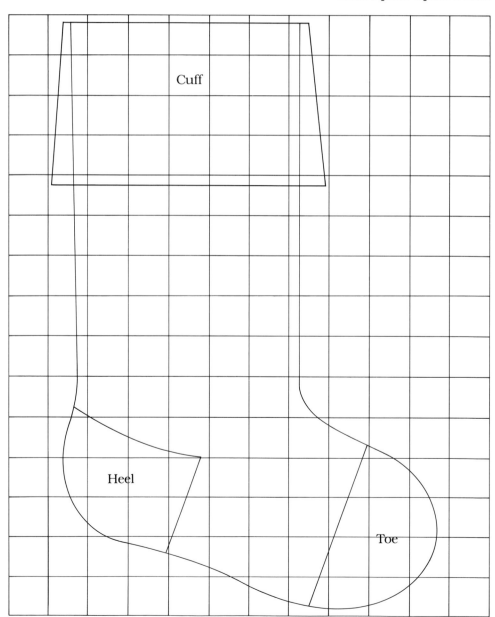

## HEART-SHAPED PLACE MATS

Make a set of country place mats and napkins for an instant decorating statement. The heart shape has always been a country design, most often used for appliqués. Red-checked homespun is almost synonymous with country, and while the fabric has a holiday feeling, these place mats can be used year-round. Each is a generous 15 × 17 inches, and you can get 3 top pieces from ½ yard of fabric. I've made them reversible, with the tops red checked and the backs red plaid. You might want to use a solid for the backing.

### Materials (for 6 place mats)

*Note:* 45- or 52-inch-wide fabric will yield 3 place mat tops per ½ yard.

1 yard red-checked homespun *or* sailcloth

1 yard red plaid or solid homespun *or* sailcloth

thin batting

tracing paper

### Directions

**1.** Enlarge the heart pattern. (See page 79.) Add ¼-inch seam allowance.

**2.** Pin the pattern to the red-checked fabric and cut out 6, adding ¼-inch seam allowance all around.

**3.** Cut 6 more hearts from solid red or plaid fabric in the same way.

**4.** Next, use the pattern to cut a heart-shaped piece of batting for each place mat. Trim the batting so that it is ½ inch smaller all around than the pattern.

**5.** With right sides facing and raw edges aligned, pin the front and back of one heart together. Starting at one side of the point, stitch around ¼ inch from edge. Leave one side edge open for turning.

**6.** Clip around curves in the seam allowance, then turn right-side-out. From the inside, push the curves and the point out. Press.

**7.** Insert the batting and smooth into place. Turn raw edges of open side in and press. Machine-stitch around outside edge.

**8.** To finish place mats, machine-stitch around heart shape ¼ inch from outer edge all around.

### To quilt (if desired):

Use a yardstick to mark a ½-inch grid diagonally across each place mat. (See page 17.) Take small running stitches along all lines.

## HEART APPLIQUE NAPKINS

Make a set of forest-green homespun napkins and add a red-checked heart appliqué to each one. It's easy and economical and will enhance your eating area—especially when paired with the heart-shaped place mats.

A small heart appliqué is stitched into one corner of each napkin. (It is the same appliqué used for the Christmas Potholder.) Consider making this project for gift-giving as well as for your own entertaining during the holidays.

### Materials (for 6 napkins, each 16 × 16 inches)

*Note:* The homespun fabric used here is 52 inches wide. Adjust amount of fabric or size of napkins for 45-inch-wide fabric.

small piece of red-checked fabric

1½ yards forest-green plaid homespun (1 yard for 4 napkins)

tracing paper

heavy paper *or* cardboard for template

### Directions

*To make napkins*

**1.** Cut 4 squares, each 16½ × 16½ inches, from green plaid.

**2.** Turn raw edges under ¼ inch all around, and press.

**3.** Fold edges under another ¼ inch, press, and stitch all around.

*To make appliqués*

**1.** Trace the heart pattern on page 73 and transfer to heavy paper or cardboard for template. (See page 14.)

**2.** Place the template on red fabric and trace around the outline 4 times with ½ inch between each one. If you want to hand-appliqué, cut out each heart with an extra ¼ inch all around. If you want to zigzag-stitch around the edges, cut out each heart on the drawn lines.

*To hand-appliqué*

**1.** In seam allowance, clip around the curves of each heart. Place the template on the back of the heart fabric and fold the edges over the template. Press with the tip of a hot iron.

**2.** Remove the template, turn the heart right-side-up and press.

**3.** Pin the appliqué in position with the point in one corner of the napkin. Slip-stitch all around.

*To machine-appliqué*

**1.** Pin the heart shape in position on the napkin.

**2.** Using red thread, zigzag-stitch around edge of the heart.

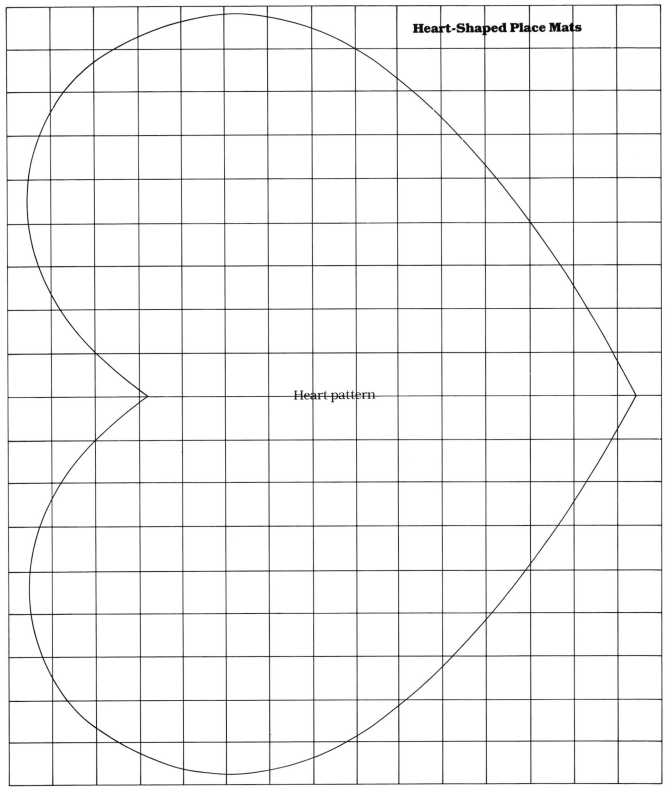

**Heart-Shaped Place Mats**

Heart pattern

Each square equals 1 inch

Add ¼ inch seam allowance

# Christmas Quilt

I've always thought it would be fun to have a Christmas quilt with matching pillows. A Christmas Star pattern seems just right for a special holiday bedcover. Made with homespun fabric in red and green checks, the background is dominated by white squares, making it light and airy. Since the design and fabrics are traditional, the project is quite appealing at any time of the year. This quilt was made to fit a double or queen-size bed and is 76 × 97 inches.

## Materials

*Note:* Yardages are figured for fabric 45 inches wide.

1 yard red-checked homespun (*A*)

2½ yards white fabric (*B*)

3 yards green-checked homespun (*C*)

5½ yards backing fabric

batting

## Directions

*Note:* All measurements include ¼ inch seam allowance.

*Cut the following:*

from red check:

    1 rectangle, 36 × 45 inches

from white:

    1 rectangle, 36 × 45 inches

    48 squares, each 5 × 5 inches

    48 squares, each 3½ × 3½ inches

    24 squares, each 4½ × 4½ inches. Cut each square into 4 triangles.

from green check:

    borders:

        2 strips, each 8½ × 60½ inches

        2 strips, each 8½ × 97½ inches

    lattice strips:

        8 strips, each 3½ × 18½ inches

        3 strips, each 3½ × 60½ inches

    12 squares, each 3½ × 3½ inches

    24 squares, each 4½ × 4½ inches. Cut each square into 4 triangles.

**1.** With right sides facing and raw edges aligned, stitch a green triangle to a white triangle along one edge to make a larger triangle. Make 96. Open seams and press.

**2.** Next, stitch 2 pieced triangles together to make a square, as shown in Figure 1. Make 48. Open seams and press.

Figure 1

**Christmas Quilt**

Figure 2. Center of block

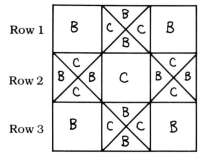

3. With right sides facing and raw edges aligned, join a small white square to a green-and-white square along one edge.
4. Next, join another white square to complete the first row of 3 squares. Open seams and press. For second row, join a green-and-white square to a green square and then complete row with a green-and-white square. For third row, repeat the first.
5. With right sides facing and raw edges aligned, join row 1 to row 2 and add row 3, as shown in Figure 2, to make a Christmas Star square. This is the center of the block.

*To make one block*

*Note:* The following directions are for the quick-and-easy right-triangle method. (See page 18.)

1. Mark 48 squares, each 5½×5½ inches, on the wrong side of the large white fabric (36×45 inches). Draw a diagonal line through all squares.
2. With right sides facing, pin to same-size piece of red-checked fabric. Stitch ¼ inch in on each side of the diagonal lines.
3. Cut on all solid lines. Open seams and press. You should have 96 squares made of red-and-white triangles.
4. Refer to Figure 3. With right sides facing and raw edges aligned, stitch squares together to make a block. Make 12 blocks.
5. Open seams and press.

*To make a row*

1. With right sides facing and raw edges aligned, join a green lattice strip (3½×18½ inches) to a block along the bottom edge. Open seams and press.
2. Continue to join blocks in this way, as shown in Figure 4, until you have 4 rows of 3 blocks each.

*To join rows and borders*

1. With right sides facing and raw edges aligned, join a green lattice strip (3½×18½ inches) to the bottom edge of the first row of blocks.
2. Continue to join rows in this way. Open seams and press.
3. With right sides facing and raw edges aligned, stitch the top and bottom border pieces to the pieced quilt top.
4. Next, join the side border pieces. Open seams and press.

*To finish*

1. Cut the batting ½ inch smaller than the quilt top all around.
2. Cut the backing fabric in half so that you have 2 pieces, each 2¾ yards. Cut one piece in half lengthwise.
3. With right sides facing and raw edges aligned, join one narrow half to each side edge of the wider fabric piece. (See page 13 for backing details.) Trim the fabric to the size of the quilt top.
4. With wrong sides facing and batting between, pin top, backing, and batting together.

**5.** Beginning in the center and moving outward in a sunburst pattern, baste the top, batting, and backing together with long stitches through all 3 layers.

**6.** To quilt by hand, take small running stitches ¼ inch in from seam line on each side of all seams.

**7.** When all quilting is complete, clip away basting stitches.

**8.** Turn raw edges of the quilt top under ½ inch and press. Turn backing edges to inside ½ inch and press. Pin edges together all around.

**9.** Stitch all around with slip-stitch or machine stitch.

Figure 3. Quilt block                                                              **Christmas Quilt**

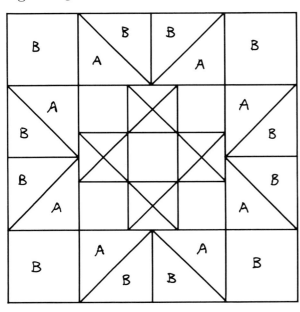

Figure 4. To make a row

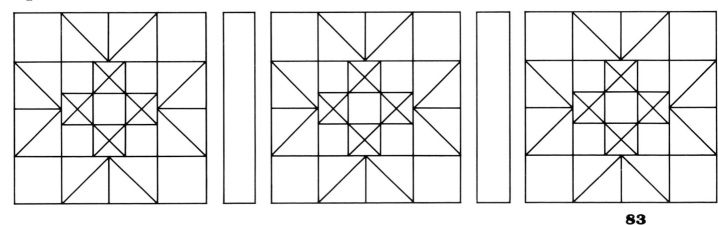

# Christmas Pillows

If you like the idea of having a patchwork Christmas decoration, but feel that the quilt is too ambitious a project, start with a Christmas pillow. This will teach you the basics of patchwork as applied to making a star design. When finished, you will have made one block of the quilt. Making a pillow top will give you an idea of how much is involved in making the Christmas quilt on page 80. Then decide whether to do just the pillow or proceed with the quilt. The finished size of each pillow is 18 × 18 inches. One is predominantly red, while the other uses green as the main color. They are trimmed with contrasting-color piping all around.

## Materials

For 1 predominantly green pillow. For a predominantly red pillow, reverse amounts of red and green homespun.
*Note:* Yardages are figured for fabric 45 inches wide.

¼ yard red-checked homespun (*A*)

⅓ yard white fabric (*B*)

⅔ yard green-checked homespun (*C*)

2 yards cording

1 pillow form, 18 × 18 inches, *or* stuffing

## Directions

*Note:* All measurements include ¼-inch seam allowance.

*Cut the following:*

from green check:
> 1 square, 18½ × 18½ inches, for the back
> 2 strips, each 1½ × 38 inches, to cover the cording
> 1 square, 3½ × 3½ inches
> 2 squares, each 4½ × 4½ inches. Cut each square into 4 triangles.

from white:
> 4 squares, each 5 × 5 inches
> 4 squares, each 3½ × 3½ inches
> 2 squares, each 4½ × 4½ inches. Cut each square into 4 triangles.
> 1 strip, 6 × 23 inches

from red check:
> 1 strip, 6 × 23 inches

**1.** With right sides facing and raw edges aligned, stitch a green triangle to a white triangle to make a larger triangle. Make 8. Open seams and press.

**2.** Next, stitch 2 pieced triangles together along the long edge to make a square, as shown in Figure 1 on page 80. Make 4. Open seams and press.

**3.** With right sides facing and raw edges aligned, stitch a small white square to a green-and-white square along one edge. Then join with a white square to make the first row for the star square, as shown in Figure 2 on page 82. For second row, join a pieced square to a green square and complete row with a pieced square. For third row, repeat the first.

**4.** Right sides together and raw edges aligned, join row 1 to row 2 and add row 3, as shown in Figure 2, to make a Christmas Star square. This is the center of the block. Open seams and press.

### To make the block

*Note:* The following directions are for the quick-and-easy right-triangle method. (See page 18.)

**1.** Mark 4 squares, each 5½ × 5½ inches, on the wrong side of 6 × 23-inch strip of white fabric. Draw a diagonal line through each square.

**2.** With right sides facing, pin this to same-size red check fabric. Stitch ¼ inch in on each side of the diagonal lines.

**3.** Cut on all solid lines. Open seams and press. You should have 8 squares made of red-and-white triangles.

**4.** With right sides facing and raw edges aligned, stitch squares together to make the block with the star in the center, as shown in Figure 3 on page 83. Open seams and press.

### To finish

**1.** Stitch the 2 green strips of fabric together along one short end to make a long strip to cover the cording.

**2.** *To make piping:* Beginning ½ inch from the end of the green fabric strip, place the cording in the center of the wrong side of the strip and fold the fabric over so that the raw edges meet. With the cording encased inside the fabric, use the zipper foot on the sewing machine to stitch as close to the cording as possible.

**3.** With right sides facing and raw edges aligned, pin the piping around the edge of the pillow top, overlapping the raw ends of the piping fabric. Stitch around, as close to cording as possible.

**4.** With right sides facing and raw edges aligned, pin the backing fabric to the top of the pillow with piping between.

**5.** Using the piping stitches as a guide, stitch around 3 sides and 4 corners, leaving enough of an opening for turning. Trim seams and clip corners. Turn right-side-out and press.

For the second pillow, reverse the colors: make the star in red and white and the surrounding squares in green and white. The piping and backing will then be made with the red-checked homespun.

# Patchwork and Appliqué Tablecloth

Using large squares of sage green, cranberry red, and white fabric, you can make this country patchwork tablecloth in no time. By adding our simple tree and wreath appliqués, you will create a one-of-a-kind table covering for a special holiday setting. The finished size is 58 × 58 inches, but you can make the tablecloth larger by adding more squares or a border all around. Each finished square is 8 × 8 inches.

## Materials

*Note:* Yardages are figured for fabric 45 inches wide.

small pieces of solid red fabric for wreath bows and berries

½ yard solid green fabric for appliqués

1 ¼ yards white fabric (*A*)

1 ¼ yards green-checked homespun (*B*)

1 ¾ yards red-checked homespun (*C*)

3 ¼ yards backing fabric (if desired)

thin batting (if quilting is desired)

tracing paper

heavy paper *or* cardboard for templates

fusible webbing

## Directions

*Note:* All measurements include ¼-inch seam allowance.

*Cut the following:*

from white (*A*):

      12 squares, each 8½ × 8½ inches

      24 squares, each 5 × 5 inches. Cut each square into 2 triangles.

from green check (*B*):

      25 squares, each 8½ × 8½ inches

from red check (*C*):

      borders:

            2 strips, each 1½ × 56½ inches, for top and bottom

            2 strips, each 1½ × 58½ inches, for sides

      12 squares, each 6⅛ × 6⅛ inches

*To make patchwork block*

**1.** With right sides facing and raw edges aligned, stitch a white (*A*) triangle to each side of red (*C*) square to make a larger square. Make 12 blocks.

**2.** Open all seams and press.

### To make rows
*Row 1*
**1.** With right sides facing and raw edges aligned, stitch a *B* square to a block. Open seams and press.
**2.** Continue to join *B* squares and blocks so that you have a row of 4 *B* squares separated by 3 blocks, as shown in Figure 1. Open seams and press. Make 4.

*Row 2*
**1.** With right sides facing and raw edges aligned, join an *A* square to a *B* square. Open seams and press.
**2.** Continue to join *A* squares to *B* squares until you have a row of 4 *A* squares separated by 3 *B* squares, as shown in Figure 1. Open seams and press. Make 3.

### To join rows
**1.** With right sides facing and raw edges aligned, stitch row 1 to row 2 along the long edge. Open seams and press.

**2.** Continue to join all 7 rows in this way, alternating row 1 and row 2, as shown in Figure 2.

### To join borders

**1.** With right sides facing and raw edges aligned, stitch the top and bottom border pieces to the patchwork top. Open seams and press.

**2.** Join the side border pieces in the same way.

### To make appliqués

**1.** Trace the wreath, bow, tree, and berry patterns. Transfer to heavy paper or cardboard for templates. (See page 14 for template details.) Cut out.

**2.** Trace around the tree and wreath templates on solid green fabric 6 times each.

**3.** Pin the fabric shapes to same-size piece of fusible webbing and cut out all appliqués.

**4.** Pin a tree in the center of the first white square, then a wreath in the next white square, continuing in this way until each white square is filled.

**5.** Using a medium-hot iron, fuse each appliqué to the fabric background by holding the iron in place for 2 to 3 seconds. Remove pins as you do this.

**6.** Using a zigzag stitch on your machine, and matching thread to fabric, stitch around all edges of each wreath and tree appliqué. The appliqués will stay in place through several washings even if they are not stitched down. When they begin to lift at the edges, simply reapply a small piece of webbing and re-iron. The edges of these appliqués, with their tiny points, are too difficult to turn and stitch by hand.

**7.** Place the bow template on the solid red fabric and trace around the outline 6 times. Place the berry template on the red fabric and draw 78 times.

**8.** Pin the red fabric with the berries and bows drawn on it to the same-size fusible webbing. Cut out all pieces.

**9.** Position the bows at the bottom of each wreath and fuse with a medium-hot iron. Arrange 3 clusters of 3 berries each around each wreath and fuse to background. Place 4 berries, evenly spaced in zigzag fashion, on each tree, as shown on pattern (see page 91). Fuse in position.

### To quilt

Since this project will be used as a tablecloth, it is not necessary to back and quilt it. At this point, you can simply turn all edges under and hem. If you want to make it more finished, you can add a backing. And, if you'd like to quilt it for a more interesting project, do as follows:

**1.** Cut the backing fabric in half so you have 2 pieces, each 1¾ yards. Cut one of the pieces in half lengthwise. (See page 13 for backing details.)

**2.** With right sides together and raw edges aligned, join one narrow half to each side edge of wider fabric piece. Trim fabric to size of quilt top.

**3.** Cut thin batting ¼ inch smaller than top piece all around.

**4.** With wrong side facing and batting between, pin top, batting, and backing together.

**5.** Beginning at the center and working outward, baste all 3 layers together with long stitches in a sunburst pattern.

**6.** If you want to quilt quickly, machine-stitch along all seam lines, stopping just before seam allowance all around.

**7.** To hand-quilt, take small running stitches ¼ inch in on both sides of each seam line.

Since the green squares are so large, consider making a pattern of quilt stitches in each one. You might like to use the tree or wreath template as a quilting design. To do this, place the template on each square and draw around the outline with a light pencil. Follow these lines with small, even stitches. When you have finished quilting, the light pencil won't be visible.

### To finish

**1.** If you want to add a backing without doing any quilting, pin the backing fabric to the top of the tablecloth with right sides facing. Stitch around all edges, leaving enough of an opening for turning. Turn right-side-out and press. Turn raw edges in and slip-stitch closed.

**2.** To finish quilted top, turn raw edges in ¼ inch and press. Turn backing edges in ¼ inch and press. Machine-stitch around outside edge to finish.

Figure 2. Joining rows

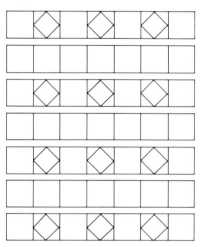

## Patchwork and Appliqué Tablecloth

Figure 1

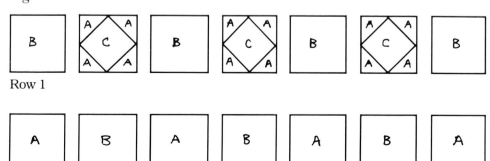

Row 1

Row 2

Berry

Bow

Wreath pattern

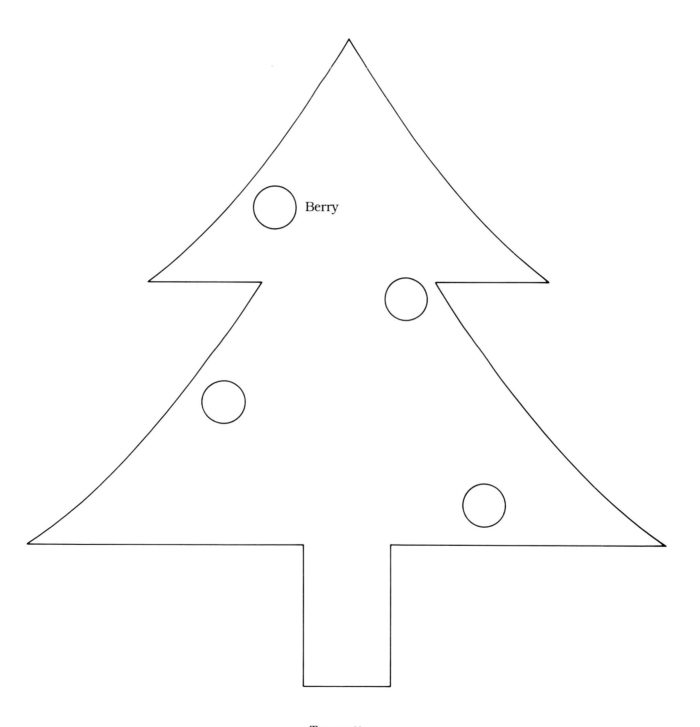

Berry

Tree pattern

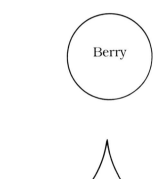

Berry

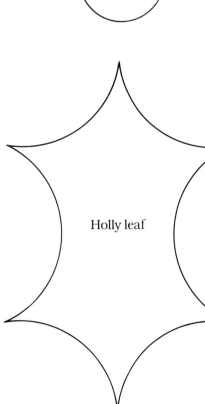

Holly leaf

# Small Gifts

Sometimes I like to add my own touches to store-bought items for last-minute gifts or for instant decorative cheer in my home. Regular white hand towels, for example, make a guest bathroom more inviting when they are trimmed with red plaid fabric and a holiday appliqué. Two of them make a thoughtful gift. Hang your guests' coats on red-and-green padded hangers, scented with pine-filled patchwork heart sachets. Cut out fabric hearts and gingerbread men, then stitch them together to create a garland to hang over a mirror, on the tree, or on the front door.

## APPLIQUED TOWELS

Buy regular guest-size towels and use scraps of fabric to make the appliqués. You can either zigzag-stitch them in place or use iron-on fusible webbing for a quick-and-easy project.

### Materials

2 white hand towels

small amounts of solid red fabric

small amounts of green-checked fabric

for each towel: red plaid strip, 4 to 6 inches deep by the width of the towel plus 1½ inches

tracing paper

heavy paper *or* cardboard for templates

fusible webbing (if desired)

### Directions

**1.** On the red plaid strip, fold all edges under ¼ inch and press.

**2.** Pin to the towel so that the bottom edge of the fabric is aligned with the bottom edge of the towel. There should be ½ inch extra on each side. Turn these edges to the back and pin.

**3.** Using red thread, stitch across the top and bottom, as close to the edge as possible. Then stitch along each side to attach fabric strip.

*To machine-stitch appliqué*

**1.** Trace holly and berry patterns and transfer to heavy paper or cardboard to make templates. (See page 14.) Cut out.

**2.** Trace around holly template on green-checked fabric 6 times.

**3.** Trace around berry template on red fabric 6 times.

**4.** Cut out all pieces.

**5.** Pin 3 holly leaves and 3 berries to each towel, as shown in photograph.

**6.** Using a zigzag stitch and matching thread, stitch around the edges of all appliqué pieces.

### No-sew appliqué

**1.** Make templates as described in step 1, page 92. Trace shapes onto fabric as described in steps 2 and 3, page 92. Do not cut out.

**2.** Pin the red berry fabric and the green holly fabric (with drawn patterns) to fusible webbing. Cut out all pieces.

**3.** Position each piece on the towel, and, using a medium-hot iron, fuse each appliqué to towel by holding iron in place for 2 to 3 seconds.

The appliqué pieces will be secure enough to go through several washings before they begin to peel away. When this happens, simply cut another piece of the webbing and reapply.

## PADDED HANGERS

Use a variety of red and green fabrics to make a set of 3 padded hangers with heart-shaped patchwork sachets. This is a thoughtful gift as well as a good bazaar item. It is also a good way to add a bit of the holiday spirit to your guest closet. What a pleasant surprise for your guests when they open the closet and find you've carried the decorations beyond the front door.

### Materials

wooden coat hangers
piece of fabric, 3 inches wide and 5 inches longer than your hangers
batting, same size as fabric
fabric scraps for the sachets
12 inches of ½-inch-wide satin ribbon for each sachet
handful of potpourri or pine needles for each sachet
stuffing
tracing paper

### Directions

**1.** Fold one long edge of the fabric under ¼ inch and press.

**2.** Wrap the batting around the wooden hanger so it is evenly padded and not too tight. There will be an extra 1½ inches of padding on each end. (See Figure 1.)

**3.** Take large, loose basting stitches across the batting to hold it in place.

**4.** Place the padded hanger on top of the wrong side of the fabric, with the raw edge of the fabric at the top.

**5.** Make a small slit on top of the fabric in front of the hook. Wrap the fabric around the batting so that the bottom, turned edge fits over the raw edge at the top.

**6.** Slit the fabric to fit the hook and turn the slit edges under.

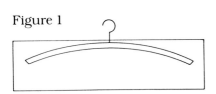

Figure 1

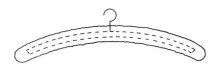

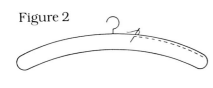

Figure 2

94

**7.** Secure the edges around the hook with a slip-stitch, drawing them together. Slip-stitch along the top fabric edge, as shown in Figure 2.
**8.** Take a small running stitch around the fabric at each end of the hanger and pull to gather the fabric loosely. Tuck excess fabric ends inside and pull stitches tight to close. Knot thread and bury end.

## PATCHWORK HEART SACHETS

**1.** Trace the full heart pattern on page 41 and cut out each section. Pin each pattern piece to a different fabric scrap and cut out, adding ¼ inch all around for seam allowance.
**2.** Following the diagram (see page 41) piece the fabrics together. Use the pieced heart as a pattern to cut one solid heart from fabric for the backing.
**3.** With right sides facing and raw edges aligned, stitch the patchwork top to the backing fabric, leaving a small opening on one side edge for turning.

Figure 1

**4.** Clip into seam allowance around all curves; turn right-side-out.
**5.** Put a small amount of stuffing into the bottom half of the heart and fill the rest with potpourri or pine needles. Slip-stitch opening closed.
**6.** Add a small ribbon bow to the top of the heart and tack the sachet in place on the front of the hanger. Refer to Figure 1.

## GARLAND TRIMMING

There are 2 ways to make this simple gingerbread-and-heart garland. One requires no sewing and is simply a cutting project that you can make in a jiffy. The other way requires cutting and stuffing, but the results are a little more interesting because you will have a 3-dimensional garland. Directions are given for both so you can make it either way.

### Materials

red and green fabric scraps
½ yard red or green ½-inch-wide satin ribbon
stuffing for 3-dimensional version
tracing paper
cardboard for templates
fusible webbing (if desired)

### Directions

*For both methods*

Before you begin, decide how long you want your garland to be and determine how many gingerbread men and hearts you will need for this length. Add enough so that they will hang in a curve rather than in a straight row.

**1.** Trace the gingerbread man and the heart patterns.

**2.** Transfer patterns to cardboard to make templates. (See page 14.)

**3.** Place the gingerbread man template on the green fabric. Using a ballpoint pen, trace around the outline to make the front piece. Leaving a ½-inch space between each one, trace another pattern for the back piece. Repeat as many times as needed. Do the same for each heart template, on the red fabric.

**4.** *For no-sew method*, pin the fabric to fusible webbing and cut out all pattern pieces. *For stitch 'n' stuff method*, cut each pattern piece with an extra ¼ inch all around.

**5.** *No-sew:* Pin the front and back pieces together with the fusible webbing between. Tack each one in the center with a medium-hot iron, removing pins as you go. Do not fuse the entire design at this time. *Stitch 'n' stuff:* With right sides facing and raw edges aligned, stitch front and back pieces together around outside edges, leaving small opening for turning. Clip around curves, turn right-side-out, and stuff tightly. Since these items are so tiny, it is helpful to use a crochet hook or similar item to push the stuffing into each one. Slip-stitch openings closed.

### To finish

*No-sew:* Beginning and ending with a gingerbread man, arrange shapes evenly, with the hearts between. Lift the side edge of each heart and slip the tip of the gingerbread man's arm between the pieces of fusible webbing. Using a medium-hot iron, fuse each piece together by holding iron in place on each cutout for 1 to 2 seconds.

*Stitch 'n' stuff:* Arrange the gingerbread men and hearts as for no-sew project and tack the tips of the gingerbread men's arms to the side edges of the hearts with small, invisible stitches.

*For both:* Cut the ribbon in half and attach at each end for hanging.

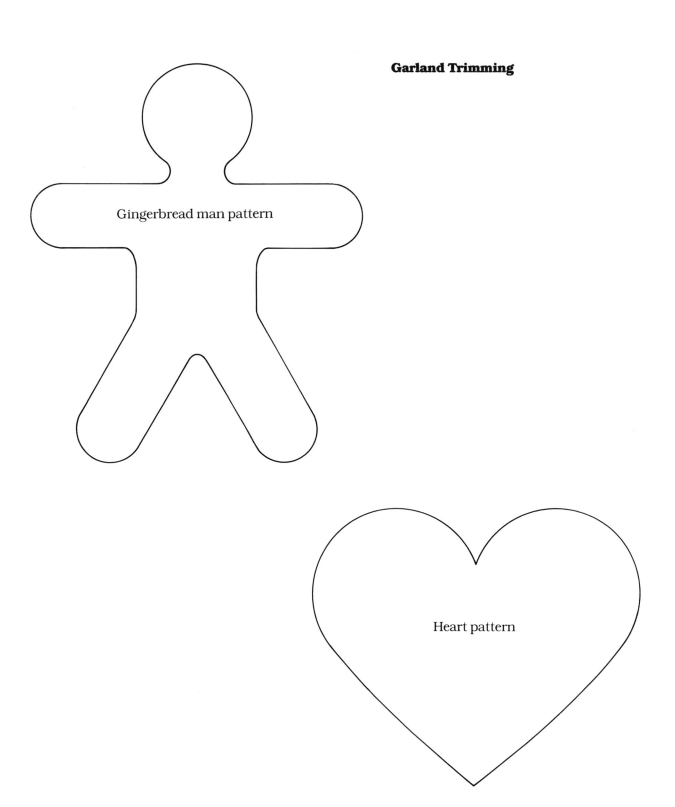

Gingerbread man pattern

Heart pattern

# Country Quilts To Treasure

**I**n this section, I've tried to present a variety of quilts that reflect different aspects of quiltmaking. They represent designs and techniques being done today. One of the quilts is an antique with a modern feeling. It is included because the bold, polka-dot design is so contemporary-looking that I thought you might enjoy reproducing it. Another old quilt was originally made from scraps of colorful fabrics. While the quilt is old, the design is one that a modern-day quilter would surely enjoy making. And who doesn't want a new project that calls for remnants? These quilts are already family heirlooms. Therefore, the ones you make using our directions will add to an American tradition!

Our quilts-to-make-in-a-weekend have been quite popular. The one included here reflects the influence of Amish designs. For this reason, it will always be treasured. The Cathedral Window pattern is more difficult than most. It is therefore hard to find one that is beautifully made. We were fortunate to find an expert who has mastered this interesting technique.

The English used floral chintz fabric to make beautiful quilts long before our early settlers began quilting. I used a pretty rose-chintz pattern for a quick-and-easy coverlet in the English tradition.

Here, too, you'll find wall hangings that represent another aspect of quiltmaking. These small-scale projects are excellent examples of how to use color with traditional patterns.

Whether you choose to make a small wall hanging or a weekend quilt, or to reproduce an antique, the making of a quilt will be a rewarding experience.

# The Weekend Quilt

Weekend quilting is an extremely popular concept. We know busy homemakers, mothers, and career women, as well as a few men, who want to make a quilt, but don't have a lot of leisure time. The idea of a "weekend quilt" came about in a class that my husband, Jon, and I were teaching. Everyone in the class was a newcomer in town and new to quilting.

We designed 19 different quilt patterns that could be pieced and machine-quilted in a weekend. If anyone wanted to hand-quilt, this would take longer, but the basic quilt could be finished and ready to use after a weekend's work.

No doubt I will never do a quilting book again that doesn't include at least one weekend quilt project. The one shown here is reminiscent of an Amish design. The patchwork is made from large triangles, rectangles, and squares. There are no pattern pieces to fuss with. The finished size is $68 \times 84$ inches, which is ample for a queen-size bed.

## Materials

*Note:* Yardages are figured for fabric 45 inches wide.

1 yard light green fabric (*A*)

1¼ yards red fabric (*B*)

1¼ yards royal blue fabric (*C*)

2½ yards dark-green fabric (*D*)

4 yards fabric for backing

batting

## Directions

*Note:* All measurements include ¼-inch seam allowance.

*Cut the following:*

from light green (*A*): 48 squares, each 2½ × 2½ inches
20 squares, each 4½ × 4½ inches
24 squares, each 5 × 5 inches. Cut each square into 2 triangles.

from red (*B*): 40 rectangles, each 2½ × 8½ inches
12 squares, each 6⅛ × 6⅛ inches

from royal blue (*C*): 31 rectangles, each 4½ × 12½ inches

from dark green (*D*):
borders:
2 strips, each 8½ × 52½ inches, for top and bottom
2 strips, each 8½ × 84½ inches, for sides

*To make one block*

**1.** With right sides facing and raw edges aligned, stitch an *A* triangle to each side of a *B* square to make a larger square. Open seams and press.

**2.** Next, stitch the long edge of a *B* rectangle to 2 opposite sides of the square you just made, as shown in Figure 1. Open seams and press.

**3.** With right sides facing and raw edges aligned, stitch a small *A* square to each short end of a *B* rectangle. Make 2. Open seams and press.

**4.** Next, stitch each of these strips to the top and bottom of the large square to make a block, as shown in Figure 1. Make 12 blocks.

**5.** Open seams and press.

*To make a row*

**1.** With right sides facing and raw edges aligned, stitch a *C* rectangle to a block along the long edge. Open seams and press.

**2.** Continue to join blocks and rectangles so that there are 3 blocks separated by 4 rectangles in a row, as shown in Figure 2. Make 4 rows.

**3.** Open all seams and press.

*To join rows*

**1.** With right sides facing and raw edges aligned, stitch an *A* large square to short end of a *C* rectangle. Open seams and press.

**2.** Continue to join 3 rectangles separated by 4 squares to make a long lattice strip. Make 5. Open seams and press.

**3.** With right sides facing and raw edges aligned, stitch a lattice strip across the top edge of a block row. Open seams and press.

**4.** Continue to join rows separated by lattice strips, as shown in Figure 3. Open seams and press.

**The Weekend Quilt**

Figure 1. To make a block

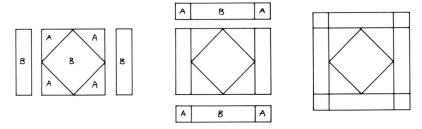

Figure 2. To make a row

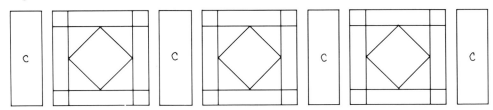

**The Weekend Quilt**

Figure 3. To join rows

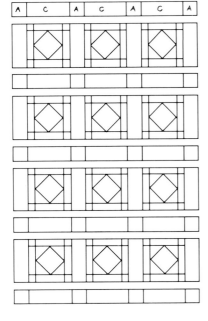

### To join borders

**1.** With right sides facing and raw edges aligned, stitch the top and bottom border strips to quilt top. Open seams and press.

**2.** Next, attach side borders in the same way.

### To finish

**1.** Cut batting ½ inch smaller than quilt top all around.

**2.** Cut the backing fabric in half so that you have 2 pieces, each 2 yards. (See page 13 for backing details.)

**3.** With right sides facing and raw edges aligned, stitch these pieces together along the long edge to create the backing. (Trim to quilt top size.)

**4.** Finish the quilt by joining front and back pieces at this point, or continue with hand- or machine-quilting. To finish now, pin backing to top piece, right sides facing. Stitch around outside edge, leaving enough of an opening for turning. Turn right-side-out, press, and machine-stitch all around top, ¼ inch from outside edge.

### To quilt

**1.** Starting at the center and moving outward in a sunburst pattern, baste the top, batting, and backing together with long stitches through all 3 layers.

**2.** To hand-quilt, begin at the center and take small running stitches ¼ inch in on both sides of each seam line. Do not stitch into seam allowance around outside edge.

**3.** To quilt by machine, quilt along all seam lines.

**4.** When all quilting is complete, clip away all basting stitches.

**5.** Fold the raw edges of the top under ¼ inch and press. Next, turn backing edges ¼ inch to the inside and press.

**6.** Stitch together with a slip-stitch or machine-stitch all around.

# Rose Coverlet

This coverlet is about $51 \times 51$ inches. It is made up of rose-patterned chintz fabric cut into 14-inch squares, which are separated by solid green lattice strips. The coverlet is perfect as a lap throw, wall hanging or table covering. It is not only good-looking, but it is also a cinch to make. If you use the lovely Waverly print pictured, you'll need only 1 yard.

## Materials

*Note:* Yardages are figured for fabric 45 inches wide.

1¼ yards rose-print chintz

1½ yards dark green fabric

1½ yards 52-inch-wide fabric for backing (dark green used here)

thin batting

## Directions

*Note:* All measurements include ¼-inch seam allowance.

*Cut the following:*

from rose print:

       9 squares, each $14 \times 14$ inches, with rose motifs centered on squares

from green:

       2 strips, each $3¼ \times 52$ inches, for side borders

       4 strips, each $3¼ \times 46½$ inches, for long lattice strips

       6 strips, each $3¼ \times 14$ inches, for short lattice strips

*To make a row*

**1.** With right sides facing and raw edges aligned, join a short lattice strip to the right side edge of a rose-print square, as shown in Figure 1. Open seams and press.

**2.** Continue by adding another square, then a short lattice strip, then another rose square to end the row, as shown in Figure 1. This completes one row of squares in the 9-square coverlet. Open seams and press.

**3.** Make 3 rows in this way.

*To join rows*

**1.** With right sides facing and raw edges aligned, stitch a long green lattice strip to the top long edge of a row. Open seams and press.

**2.** Continue to add lattice strips and rows alternately, right sides facing, ending with a fourth lattice strip, as shown in Figure 2. Open seams and press.

**3.** With right sides facing and raw edges aligned, stitch side border strips to the patchwork top. Open seams and press.

### To quilt

**1.** Cut the batting ½ inch smaller than the top all around.

**2.** If you are using 52-inch-wide fabric for the backing, you do not need to seam backing. If your fabric is 45 inches wide, you need to add a strip of fabric, 7 × 52 inches. (See page 13 for backing details.)

**3.** Pin the top piece to the batting and secure by tacking here and there in the seam lines where the squares and lattice strips meet. If you want to quilt the entire top, begin at the center and work outward, basting the top, batting, and backing together with long stitches through all 3 layers.

**4.** For quick quilting, machine-stitch along seam lines of each square and lattice strip. To hand-quilt, take small running stitches ¼ inch in on both sides of the seam lines. Do not stitch into the seam allowance around the outer edges.

**5.** When all quilting is complete, clip away basting stitches.

### To finish

**1.** If you have not done any quilting, simply pin the backing to the top piece with right sides together. Stitch around all sides, leaving a few inches open for turning. Turn right-side-out, press, and slip-stitch opening closed.

**2.** Once you've quilted the entire top, fold the raw edges of the front under ¼ inch and press. Turn backing edges to the inside ¼ inch and press.

**3.** Stitch together with a slip-stitch or machine-stitch all around.

### To hang

Sew a strip of Velcro® to the top and bottom back edges. Measure carefully; apply a corresponding strip to the wall and press in position.

**Rose Coverlet**

Figure 2. To join rows

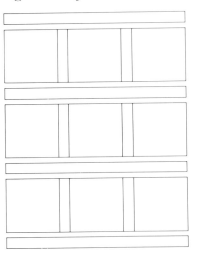

Figure 1. To make a row

# Sailboat Quilt

Each block of this delightful quilt contains a sailboat motif made from rectangles, triangles, and squares. The original full-size quilt was hand-quilted by Ginnie Beaulieu and is used in a guest room of her home on Nantucket Island. The finished size is 60 × 84 inches. This quilt is made from red, white, blue, and green solids and calicos.

## Materials

*Note:* Yardages are figured for fabric 45 inches wide.

¼ yard green calico (A)

¼ yard red calico (B)

1 yard white fabric (C)

1¾ yards blue fabric (D)

1¾ yards blue gingham

3½ yards fabric for backing

batting

tracing paper

## Directions

*Note:* All measurements include ¼-inch seam allowance.

*Cut the following:*

from green calico (A):

> 8 rectangles, each 3 × 10½ inches

from red calico (B):

> 16 squares, each 3½ × 3½ inches. Cut each square into 2 triangles.

from white (C):

> 7 squares, each 10½ × 10½ inches
> 16 rectangles, each 3 × 5½ inches
> 24 squares, each 3½ × 3½ inches. Cut each square into 2 triangles.

from blue (D):

> borders:
>> 2 strips, each 5½ × 58½ inches, for sides
>> 2 strips, each 5½ × 60½ inches, for top and bottom
> lattices:
>> 4 strips, each 2½ × 34½ inches
>> 10 strips, each 2½ × 10½ inches
> 8 rectangles, each 3 × 5½ inches
> 8 squares, each 3½ × 3½ inches. Cut each square into 2 triangles.

from blue gingham:

> borders:
>> 2 strips, each 8½ × 58½ inches, for sides
>> 2 strips, each 8½ × 60½ inches, for top and bottom

## To make a sailboat block

**1.** With right sides facing and raw edges aligned, stitch a red *B* triangle to a white *C* triangle along the diagonal to make a square. Open seams and press. Make 4.

**2.** Next, stitch all 4 squares together as shown in Figure 1. Open seams and press.

**3.** With right sides facing and raw edges aligned, stitch a *C* rectangle to each side of the large pieced square along one long edge. See Figure 1. Open seams and press. This is the top half of the block.

**4.** With right sides facing and raw edges aligned, stitch a *C* triangle to a blue *D* triangle along the diagonal to make a pieced square. Open seams and press. Make 2.

**5.** Next, stitch one white-and-blue square to each short edge of a *D* rectangle, as shown in Figure 2. Open seams and press.

**6.** With right sides facing and raw edges aligned, stitch this strip to a green calico *A* rectangle along one long edge, as shown in Figure 2. Open seams and press. This is the bottom half of the block.

**7.** With right sides facing and raw edges aligned, stitch the top half to the bottom half of the block, as shown in Figure 3. Open seams and press. Make 8 blocks.

## To make rows

### Row 1

**1.** With right sides facing and raw edges aligned, join a block to a *D* short lattice strip along the long edge. Open seams and press.

**2.** On other side of lattice strip, continue by joining a *C* large square, another short lattice strip, and then another block, as shown in Figure 4. Open seams and press. Make 3.

### Row 2

**1.** With right sides facing and raw edges aligned, stitch a *C* large square to a short lattice strip along one long edge. Open seams and press.

**2.** On other side of lattice strip, continue by joining a block, another short lattice strip, followed by another *C* square, as shown in Figure 4. Open seams and press. Make 2.

## To join rows

**1.** With right sides facing and raw edges aligned, join row 1 to a long blue lattice strip along a long edge. Open seams and press.

**2.** Continue to add lattice strips and rows in sequence, alternating row 1 and row 2 and ending with row 1, as shown in Figure 5. Open seams and press.

## To join borders

**1.** With right sides facing and raw edges aligned, stitch the blue side border strips to the sides of the quilt top. Open seams and press.

**2.** Next, join blue gingham border strips to each side in the same way. Open seams and press.

**3.** With right sides facing and raw edges aligned, stitch blue border strips to the top and bottom of the quilt top. Open seams and press.

**4.** Join remaining blue gingham border strips to top and bottom edges of the quilt.

### To quilt

**1.** Trace the quilting pattern (see page 111) and transfer to the large white squares. (See page 13 for details on transferring.)

**2.** Cut batting ½ inch smaller than quilt top all around.

**3.** Cut the backing fabric in half so that you have 2 pieces, each 1¾ yards. (See page 13 for backing details.)

**4.** With right sides facing and raw edges aligned, stitch the 2 pieces together along one long edge to create the backing. Trim to quilt top size.

**5.** Beginning at the center and moving outward in a sunburst pattern, baste the top, batting, and backing together with long stitches through all 3 layers.

**6.** Begin to quilt at the center, taking small running stitches ¼ inch in on both sides of each seam line and following the lines of the quilting pattern in each white square. Do not stitch into seam allowance around quilt top.

### To finish

**1.** When all quilting is complete, remove basting stitches.

**2.** Fold the raw edges of the top under ¼ inch and press. Turn backing edges ¼ inch to inside and press.

**3.** Stitch together with a slip-stitch or machine-stitch all around.

Detail: Sailboat Quilt

## Sailboat Quilt

Figure 1. Top half of block

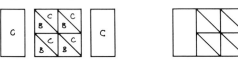

Figure 2. Bottom half of block

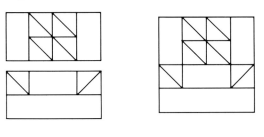

Figure 3. Sailboat block

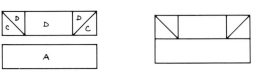

Figure 4. To make rows

Row 1

Row 2

Figure 5. To join rows

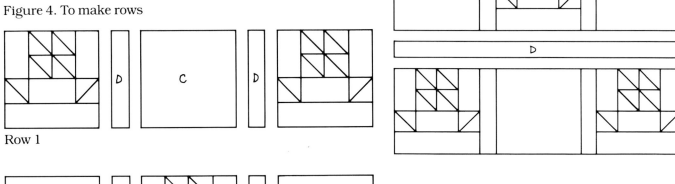

**110**

**Sailboat Quilt**

Quilting pattern

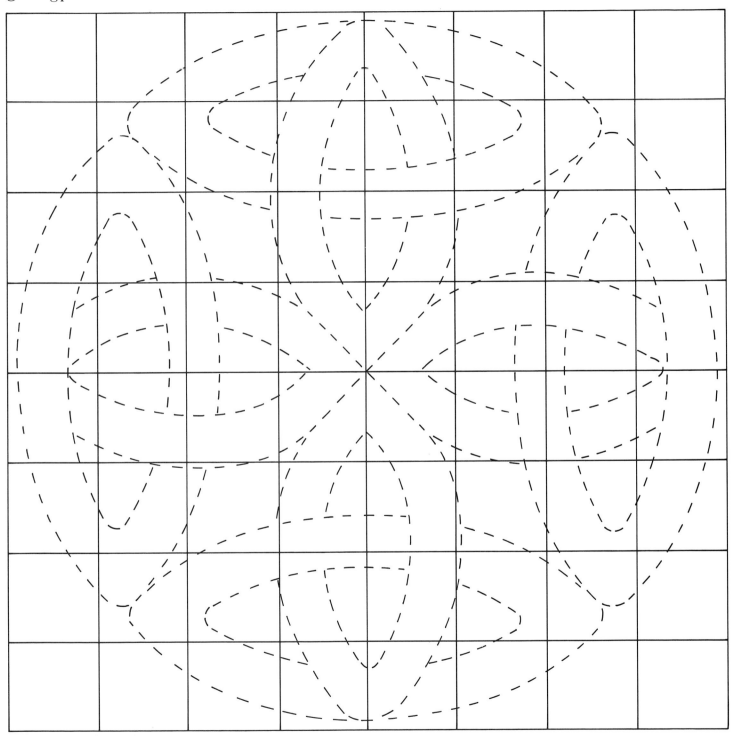

Each square equals 1 inch

# Tumbling Blocks

This is 2-year-old Emma Jane Detmer's favorite quilt. Her mother, Margaret, made it for her crib. Someday, perhaps, Emma will pass it on to her daughter. This whimsical pattern got its name for obvious reasons. The one-patch pattern is assembled in such a way as to look like 3-dimensional blocks. The finished size is 53 × 65 inches.

## Materials

*Note:* Yardages are figured for fabric 45 inches wide.

¼ yard each solid dark fabrics (rust, purple, navy, royal blue, green)

¼ yard each mediums (rose, blue, peach, lavender, gray)

½ yard each light calicos and solids (white, light pink, light blue)

1¾ yards light blue fabric, for inside borders

2 yards royal blue fabric, for outside borders

3 yards lavender fabric, for backing and outside borders

thin batting

tracing paper

cardboard for templates

pencil

## Directions

*Note:* All measurements include ¼-inch seam allowance.

*Cut the following:*

from light blue:
   borders:
      2 strips, each 2¼ × 42½ inches, for top and bottom
      2 strips, each 2¼ × 58½ inches, for sides

from royal blue:
   borders:
      2 strips, each 4 × 42½ inches, for top and bottom
      2 strips, each 4 × 64½ inches, for sides

Use the remaining fabric from both blue fabrics to cut the light and dark patch pieces.

Trace the pattern for each template and transfer to cardboard. (See page 14.) Cut out. Place the templates on the appropriate fabrics and trace around each one as necessary.

*Cut the following:*

from light solids and prints (A):
   44 from Template 1
   12 from Template 2. Cut 1 in half vertically.
   8 from Template 3

Detail: Tumbling Blocks

from medium solids (B):
54 from Template 1
from dark solids (C):
54 from Template 1

***To make a block*** (Refer to Figure 1)

**1.** With right sides facing and raw edges aligned, stitch a medium B diamond shape to a dark C diamond, as shown in Figure 1a. Open seams and press.

**2.** Next, pin a light A diamond in place, as shown in Figure 1b. Stitch. (See page 14 for details on sewing points.) Open seams and press. Make 44.

**3.** Make 6 blocks, using the A horizontal half-diamond (Template 2). See Figure 1c.

**4.** Make 4 half-blocks, using a B diamond and an A vertical half-diamond (Template 3). Make 4 half-blocks, using a C diamond and an A vertical half-diamond (Template 3). See Figure 1d. Open seams and press.

***To join blocks*** (Refer to Figure 2)

**1.** With right sides facing and raw edges aligned, join 6 blocks together, with the B diamonds on the left and the C diamonds on the right. See Figure 2a. Make 4 full rows. Open seams and press.

**2.** Next, join 5 blocks together with a half-block at each end, as shown in Figure 2b. Make 4 rows in this way. Open seams and press.

**3.** With right sides facing and raw edges aligned, join the 6 blocks made with the horizontal half-diamonds. This is the top row, as shown in Figure 3. Open seams and press.

***To join rows***

**1.** With right sides facing and raw edges aligned, stitch the top row to a row made from 5 blocks with a half-block at each end. Open seams and press.

**2.** Continue to join rows, alternating the rows of 6 full blocks with the rows made from 5 blocks with half-blocks at each end. See Figure 3 for placement. Open seams and press.

**3.** With right sides facing and raw edges aligned, stitch the remaining A (Template 2) pieces to the bottom edge. Stitch the 2 half-pieces to the bottom corners, as shown in Figure 3. Open seams and press.

***To join borders***

**1.** With right sides facing and raw edges aligned, stitch the light blue top and bottom border strips to the top and bottom edges of the quilt. Open seams and press.

**2.** Join side pieces in the same way.

**3.** With right sides facing and raw edges aligned, join the royal blue top and bottom border strips to the top and bottom edges of the quilt. Open seams and press.

**4.** Join side pieces in the same way.

*To quilt*

**1.** Trace the border quilting pattern, and, using a light pencil, transfer it to the border of the quilt. (See page 13 for details on transferring.)

**2.** Cut the backing fabric in half so that you have 2 pieces, each 1½ yards. (See page 13 for backing details.) With right sides facing, stitch the 2 backing pieces together along one long edge. Open seams and press.

**3.** Trim backing fabric so that it is 1 to 2 inches larger than quilt top all around.

**4.** Trim batting to same size as the pieced quilt top.

**5.** With wrong sides facing and batting between, pin the 3 layers together with the extra backing fabric even all around.

**6.** Beginning at the center and working outward in a sunburst pattern, take long basting stitches through all 3 layers.

**7.** Take small running stitches ¼ inch in on each side of all seam lines of the tumbling blocks. Stitch along all marked quilt lines in the borders as well.

*To finish*

**1.** Remove all basting stitches. Light pencil lines will not show.

**2.** Turn raw edges of the backing forward ¼ inch and press. Turn the remaining fabric over onto the front of the quilt top and pin all around. Slip-stitch this border to the front of the quilt.

**Tumbling Blocks**

Figure 1. To make blocks

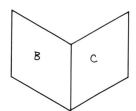

Figure 1a.

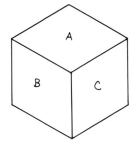

Figure 1b. Make 44

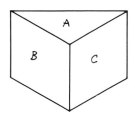

Figure 1c. Make 6

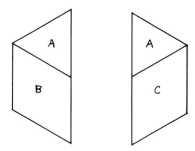

Figure 1d. Make 4 of each

**115**

**Tumbling Blocks**

Figure 2. To join blocks

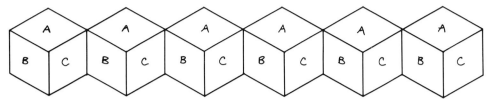

Figure 2a. Make 4

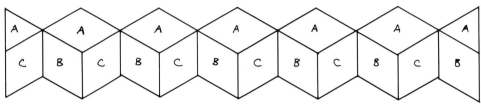

Figure 2b. Make 4

Figure 3

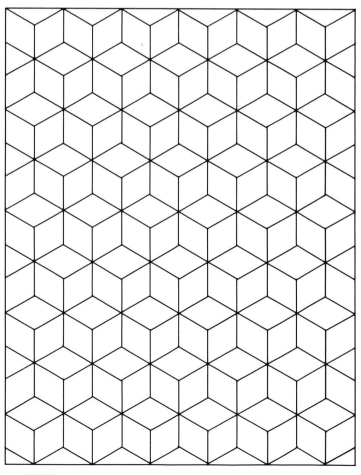

**116**

**Tumbling Blocks**

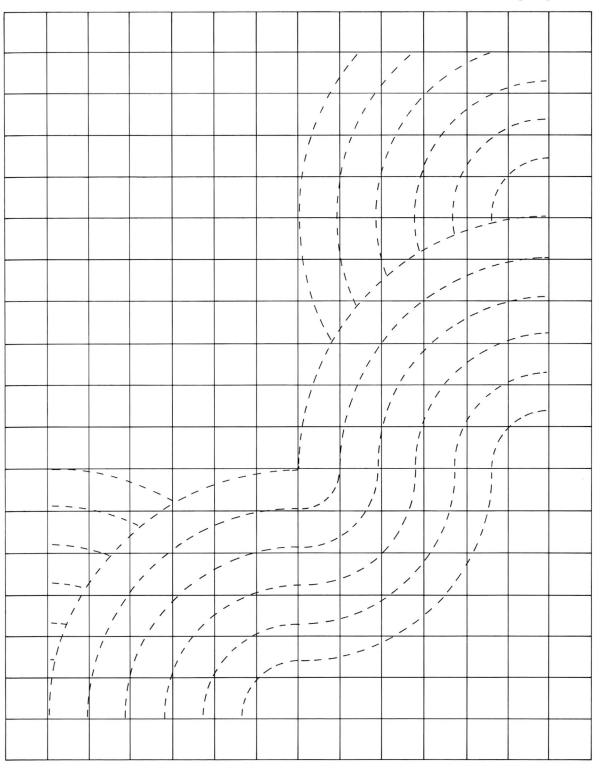

**Each square equals 1 inch**

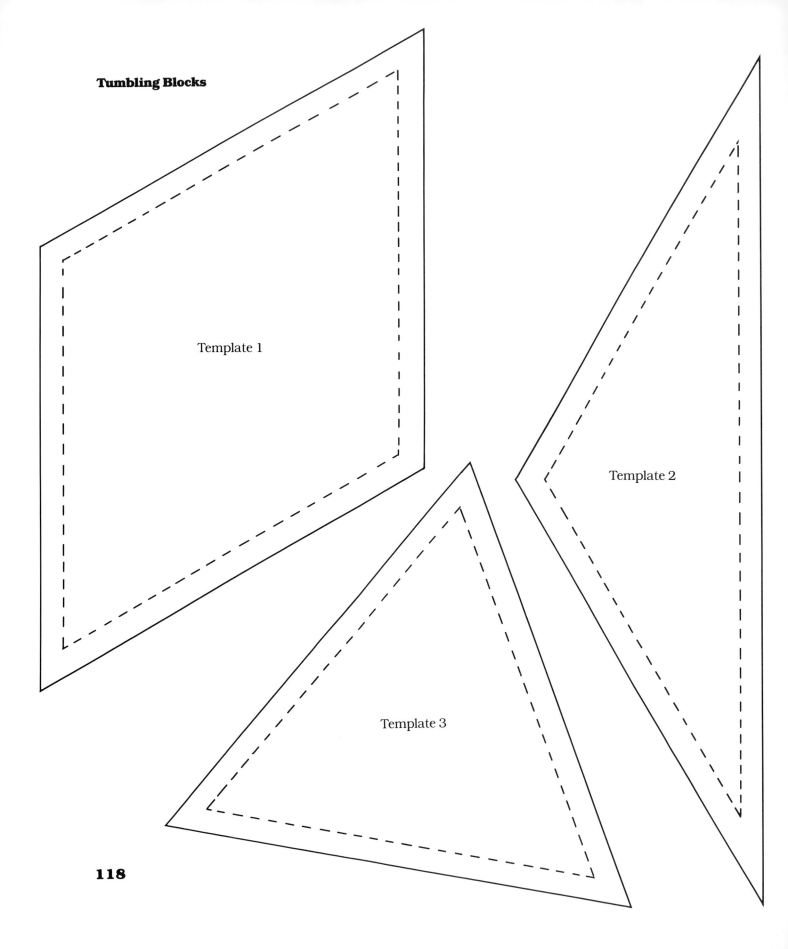

**Tumbling Blocks**

Template 1

Template 2

Template 3

118

# Sunshine and Shadow

Sunshine and Shadow is a typical Amish pattern, and, when made as a wall hanging, is quite dramatic. Working together, Margaret Detmer and Susan Fernald Joyce used the piece-stripping method to make identical projects. (See page 121.) They chose different borders, however, and it's interesting to see the same design framed differently. Susan made the one with the purple border and Maggie's border is blue with purple corners. Maggie's is slightly larger. Susan and Maggie chose different quilting designs as well, and the hand-quilting on each quilt is beautifully done. Maggie's wall hanging is about 4 feet square, and Susan's is slightly smaller.

## Materials

*Note:* Yardages are figured for fabric 45 inches wide.

### Quilt # 1
¼ yard of each color: *A, C, F, G, H, I*
1½ yards *D*, for quilt top, backing, and outer border
⅔ yard *B*
¾ yard *E*

### Quilt #2
¼ yard of each color: *C, D, F, G, H, I*
1¼ yards *A*, for quilt top and side borders
⅓ yard *B*
¾ yard *E*
backing material (any color)

### For each quilt:
1½ yards thin batting
pencil

## Directions

*Note:* All measurements include ¼-inch seam allowance.

### Cut the following:
Using the full 45-inch width of fabric, cut 2 strips, each 2½ inches wide, from each color.

from *E*:
>2 squares, each 19 × 19 inches. Cut each square on the diagonal to make 4 triangles.

## Sunshine and Shadow

### Figure 1

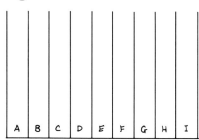

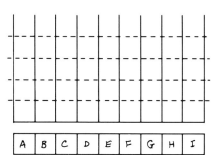

### Figure 2

| | | | | | | | |
|---|---|---|---|---|---|---|---|
| Row 1 | A | B | C | D | E | F | G |
| Row 2 | B | C | D | E | F | G | H |
| Row 3 | C | D | E | F | G | H | I |
| Row 4 | D | E | F | G | H | I | A |
| Row 5 | E | F | G | H | I | A | B |
| Row 6 | F | G | H | I | A | B | C |
| Row 7 | G | H | I | A | B | C | D |

Lower right section

### Figure 3

| | | | | | | |
|---|---|---|---|---|---|---|
| Row 1 | G | F | E | D | C | B |
| Row 2 | H | G | F | E | D | C |
| Row 3 | I | H | G | F | E | D |
| Row 4 | A | I | H | G | F | E |
| Row 5 | B | A | I | H | G | F |
| Row 6 | C | B | A | I | H | G |
| Row 7 | D | C | B | A | I | H |

Lower left section

**120**

### Quilt #1

from C—inside border:
   2 strips, each $1\frac{1}{2} \times 37\frac{1}{4}$ inches, for sides
   2 strips, each $1\frac{1}{2} \times 39\frac{1}{2}$ inches, for top and bottom
from B—outside border:
   2 strips, each $3\frac{1}{4} \times 39\frac{1}{4}$ inches, for sides
   2 strips, each $3\frac{1}{4} \times 44\frac{3}{4}$ inches, for top and bottom
from D—backing and $\frac{1}{2}$-inch border trim:
   $1\frac{1}{4}$ yards

### Quilt #2

from A—border:
   4 strips, each $6 \times 37\frac{1}{4}$ inches, for all sides
from B—corners:
   4 squares, each $6 \times 6$ inches

### For either quilt (Refer to Figure 1)

**1.** With right sides facing and raw edges aligned, pin all strips together in the sequence shown. To keep the unit from curving, stitch each strip in the opposite direction and press after each addition.
**2.** Measure and draw lines across the strips every $2\frac{1}{2}$ inches. You will need 24 strips made of 9 colors each. Cut along all horizontal lines.

### To join rows (Refer to Figure 2)

**1.** Beginning with row 1, remove the H and I squares from one strip by pulling out the thread that joins them to the row.
**2.** Remove the A square from row 2 in the same way, and join it to the I square in row 4.
**3.** Next, remove the A and B squares from row 3 and add them to the I square in row 5.
**4.** Continue moving squares on each row until you have 7 rows of 7 squares in the layout, as shown in Figure 2.
**5.** Refer to Figure 3. Complete rows for the lower left section of the quilt, as shown. Press all seams to one side.
**6.** With right sides facing and raw edges aligned, making sure that all seams match where they will be joined, stitch the lower left section to the lower right section, as shown in Figure 4.
**7.** Complete upper section in the same way, following layout shown in Figure 5 for positioning squares.
**8.** With right sides facing and raw edges aligned, matching all seams where they will be joined, stitch upper and lower sections together. Open seams and press.

### To assemble quilt top

**1.** With right sides facing and raw edges aligned, join an E triangle along each long edge to each side of the pieced center square, as shown in Figure 5.

**2.** Open seams and press.

*To join borders for quilt #1* (Refer to Figure 6)

**1.** With right sides facing and raw edges aligned, stitch *C* side borders to each side of the quilt top. Open seams and press.

**2.** Repeat at top and bottom of quilt.

**3.** With right sides facing and raw edges aligned, attach outside *B* border strips in the same way.

*To join borders for quilt #2*

**1.** With right sides facing and raw edges aligned, join a *B* square to each short end of an *A* strip, as shown in Figure 7. Open seams and press. Make 2.

**2.** With right sides facing and raw edges aligned, join the 2 remaining *A* strips to each side of the quilt top. Open seams and press.

**3.** With right sides facing and raw edges aligned, stitch the top and bottom border strips to the quilt top. Open seams and press.

*To quilt*

Each quilt has a quilting design for the *E* triangles plus a border design. See pages 124 and 125. Choose the design you prefer; then enlarge it, and, using a water-soluble marker, transfer it onto the fabric in position. (See page 13 for enlarging details.)

*For quilt #1*

**1.** Trim the quilt batting to the same size as the quilt top.

**2.** Trim the backing to 1 inch larger than the quilt top all around.

**3.** With wrong sides facing and batting between, pin all 3 layers together. Beginning at the center and working outward in a sunburst pattern, take long basting stitches through all 3 layers.

**4.** Take small running stitches along all premarked quilting lines. Do the same ¼ inch in on each side of all seam lines in each square.

*For quilt #2*

**1.** Trim batting ½ inch smaller than quilt top all around.

**2.** Trim backing to same size as quilt top.

**3.** Baste and stitch in the same way as for quilt #1, but do not stitch into seam allowance around all edges.

*To finish*

**1.** When all quilting is complete, remove basting stitches.

**2.** Turn raw edges of backing forward ¼ inch and press.

**3.** Turn remaining fabric over the raw edges onto the front of the quilt and slip-stitch all around.

**Sunshine and Shadow**

Figure 4

| G | F | E | D | C | B |
|---|---|---|---|---|---|
| H | G | F | E | D | C |
| I | H | G | F | E | D |
| A | I | H | G | F | E |
| B | A | I | H | G | F |
| C | B | A | I | H | G |
| D | C | B | A | I | H |

Lower left section

| A | B | C | D | E | F | G |
|---|---|---|---|---|---|---|
| B | C | D | E | F | G | H |
| C | D | E | F | G | H | I |
| D | E | F | G | H | I | A |
| E | F | G | H | I | A | B |
| F | G | H | I | A | B | C |
| G | H | I | A | B | C | D |

Lower right section

Figure 5

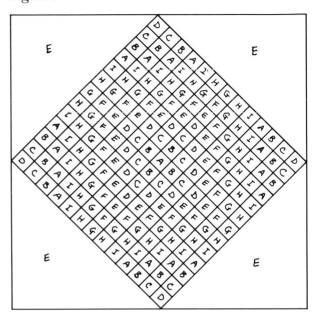

Figure 6

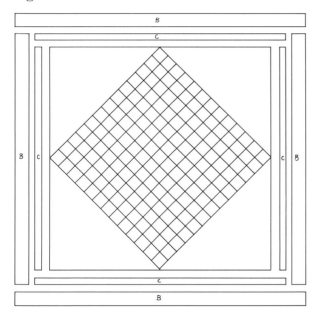

Figure 7

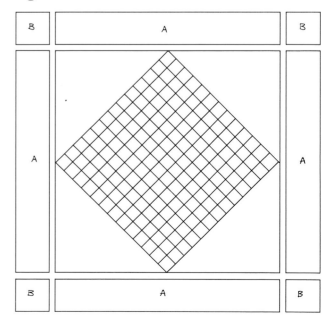

**123**

**Sunshine and Shadow**

Quilt 1 Quilting pattern

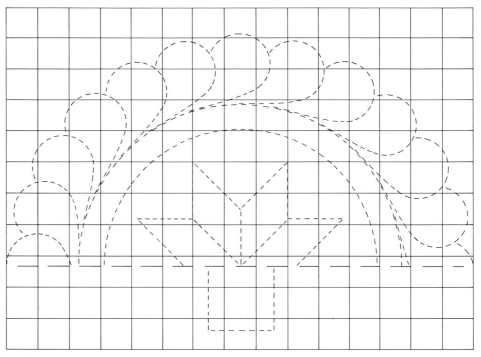

**Each square equals 1 inch**

Quilt 1 Border pattern

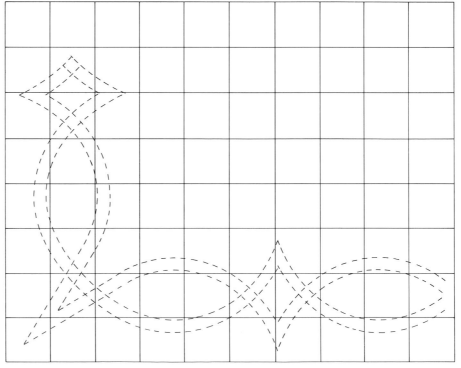

124

**Each square equals 1 inch**

**Sunshine and Shadow**

Quilt 2 Quilting pattern

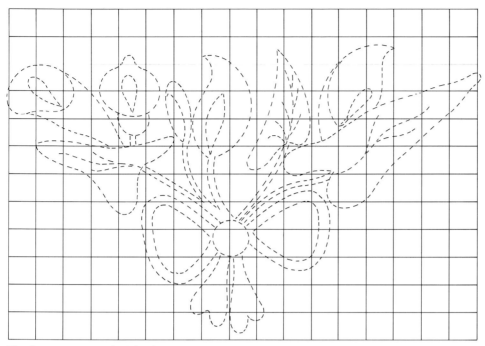

Each square equals 1 inch

Quilt 2 Border pattern

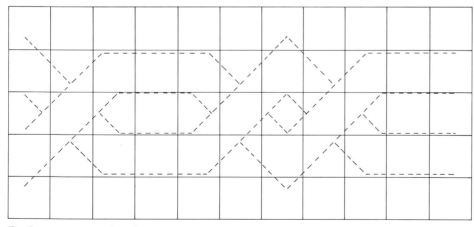

Each square equals 1 inch

# Scrap Quilt

If you've been saving scraps of fabric and have a basket full of colorful prints, this is the project for you. Imagine making a quilt that costs nothing! Each block is put together with the fabrics in no particular order. Whatever fabrics you use, you can't miss with this design. If you don't have enough scraps, buy remnants of ¼ yard each.

This 61 × 73-inch quilt is an antique that has been repaired in several places where it was worn or torn. It's easy to do with a quilt like this, because you simply add a patch of any fabric. If you own or find an old quilt that isn't in the best condition, don't discard it. Most quilts are worth patching and saving.

## Materials

fabric scraps (if purchasing remnants, buy a variety of lights and darks), including 1 yard of solids

3½ yards fabric for backing

8 yards 1-inch-wide double-fold bias binding *or* strips of fabric for the border all around quilt

thin batting

## Directions

*Note:* All measurements include ¼-inch seam allowance.

When you are cutting up squares to make triangles, choose any scraps of fabric. Usually, when I give quilt directions, I assign a letter to each piece of fabric in order to indicate color and placement. For this project, the letters indicate the size of the piece and its placement, since it doesn't matter what color or print you choose. I do, however, recommend that the 4 A triangles attached to the center D squares be the same color. Also, these triangles seem to look best when cut from solid rather than printed fabric.

*Cut the following:*

for *A*:

      120 squares, each 4 × 4 inches. Cut each square into 2 triangles.

      60 solid color squares, each 4 × 4 inches. Cut each square into 2 triangles (for use with *D* center square).

for *B*:

      120 squares, each 4 × 4 inches. Cut each square into 2 triangles.

for *C*:

      120 squares, each 3½ × 3½ inches

for *D*:

      30 squares, each 4¾ × 4¾ inches, for center squares

**1.** With right sides facing and raw edges aligned, join a solid *A* triangle along the long edge to one side of center *D* square. Open seams and press.

**2.** Stitch 3 more solid *A* triangles to the remaining sides of *D* square, as shown in Figure 1. Open seams and press. Make 30.

**3.** With right sides facing and raw edges aligned, stitch any *A* triangle to any *B* triangle along the diagonal to make a square. Open seams and press. Make 240.

**4.** With right sides facing and raw edges aligned, stitch an *A/B* square to another *A/B* square, as shown in Figure 1. Open seams and press. Make 120. (I will call these double *A/B* pieces.)

### *To make a block*

**1.** With right sides facing and raw edges aligned, stitch a *C* square to the short edge of a double *A/B* piece, then add another *C* square on the other side of the double *A/B* piece, as shown in row 1 of Figure 1. Open seams and press.

**2.** With right sides facing and raw edges aligned, stitch the long edge of a double *A/B* piece to one side of the center square, then add another double *A/B* piece to the other side of the center square, as shown in row 2 of Figure 1. Open seams and press.

**3.** With right sides facing and raw edges aligned, join a *C* square, then a double *A/B* piece, followed by a *C* square, as shown in row 3 of Figure 1.

**4.** With right sides facing and raw edges aligned, join row 1 and row 2 along the long edge. Open seams and press. Join the third row in the same way to finish the quilt block, as shown in Figure 2. Open seams and press. Make 30.

**Scrap Quilt**

Figure 1. To make a block

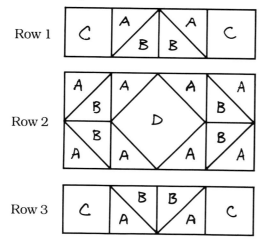

Figure 2. Quilt block

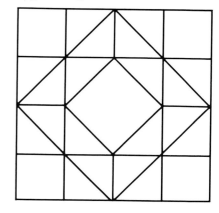

**To make rows** (Refer to Figure 3)

**1.** With right sides facing and raw edges aligned, join 2 blocks along one side edge. Open seams and press.

**2.** Continue to join blocks to make a row of 5 blocks. Make 6 rows of 5 blocks each.

**To join rows** (Refer to Figure 3)

**1.** Arrange the 6 rows horizontally and move them around to create the most pleasing sequence. With right sides facing and raw edges aligned, stitch the first 2 rows together along one long edge. Open seams and press.

**2.** Continue to join rows in this way.

**To quilt**

**1.** Cut backing fabric in half so that you have 2 pieces of fabric, each 1¾ yards long. (See page 13 for backing details.)

**2.** With right sides facing and raw edges aligned, stitch the backing fabric together along one long edge. Open seams and press.

**3.** With wrong side facing up, spread out the backing with the seam running horizontally rather than vertically. Pin the batting and quilt top over this; trim backing and batting to same size as quilt top.

**4.** Beginning in the center and working outward in a sunburst pattern, baste the top, batting, and backing together with long stitches through all 3 layers. (See page 16 for quilting details.)

**5.** To hand-quilt, take small running stitches through all 3 layers, ¼ inch in on both sides of each seam line. To machine-quilt, stitch along all seam lines.

**To finish**

**1.** When all quilting is complete, remove basting stitches.

**2.** *Bias binding:* Pin the binding around the raw edges of the quilt so that you have a ½-inch border on the front and back. Machine-stitch or slip-stitch the edges on both sides all around.

**3.** *Fabric borders:* You can use any of the fabric colors that were used in the quilt top. A dark border, such as navy blue, will look best for framing the pieced top. Cut and piece together 2 strips, each 1½ × 73½ inches, one for each side, and 2 strips, 1½ × 61½ inches, one each for the top and bottom.

**4.** Turn all long edges of each border strip under ¼ inch and press.

**5.** With wrong sides facing, fold each strip in half lengthwise and press, making each piece ½ inch wide.

**6.** Pin the top and bottom border strips over the raw edges of the quilt top so that you have a ½-inch border all around the front and back. Machine-stitch or slip-stitch.

**7.** Turn the short, raw ends of the side border strips under ¼ inch and press. Pin and stitch to the side edges of the quilt, as you did for the top and bottom.

# Cathedral Window Quilt

"I'd like to show you my quilt," said Ginnie Beaulieu, my Nantucket neighbor. I knew that she had been working on a quilt for a long time, but had no idea what an accomplished quilter she was until I saw this magnificent hand-stitched Cathedral Window quilt. Made by folding squares of plain material to frame a colored or printed fabric, this design is often known as the Stained Glass pattern. All the squares are made individually and then stitched together. "I've been working on it for a year," Ginnie told me. Be warned that this is a project to do over an extended period of time, with smaller projects in between.

You will need more than 15 yards of fabric. For this reason, many quilters choose inexpensive muslin (or "ecology cloth," as it is sometimes called) for the background. Ginnie, who is a graduate of the Rhode Island School of Design, is an accomplished artist with a good eye for design. She chose the red-and-white color scheme for a bold, graphic effect.

If you're not sure about finishing such an ambitious project, make the little Cathedral Window Pin Pillow on page 28 to try out the pattern. Go on to make a pillow and, before you know it, you'll be started on a full-size quilt. This one is $60 \times 76$ inches, which fits a double bed.

## Materials

*Note:* Yardages are figured for fabric 45 inches wide.

2½ yards red fabric

12¾ yards unbleached muslin

## Directions

*Note:* All measurements include ¼-inch seam allowance.

*Cut the following:*

from red:

　　472 squares, each 2¾ × 2¾ inches

from white:

　　252 squares, each 9 × 9 inches

*To make a square* (Refer to Figure 1)

**1.** Place a muslin square wrong-side-up. Fold each side in ¼ inch and press.

**2.** Fold each corner in to the center, as shown in Figures 1a and 1b. Sew centers together by hand.

**3.** Next, fold new corners in to the center again and secure them firmly with a cross-stitch (see Figures 1c and 1d). Make 2.

**4.** With right sides facing and raw edges aligned, join the 2 folded squares along one edge, using an overcast stitch.

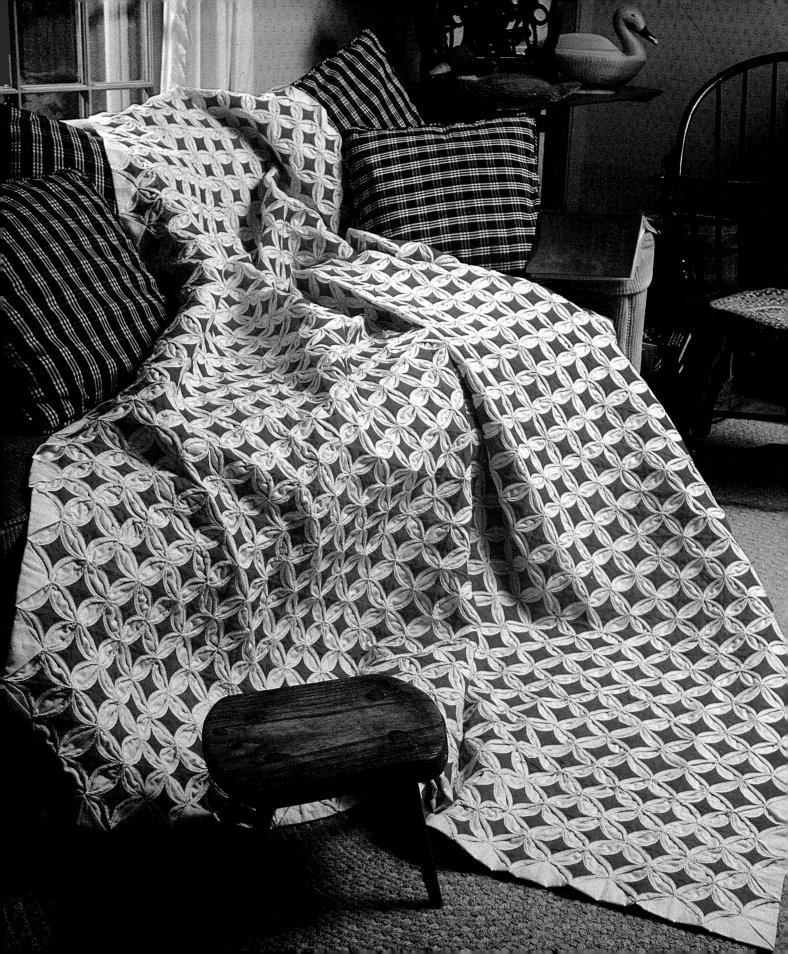

**5.** Center a red square over the overcast seam of the joined, folded squares, with opposite points of red square on upper and lower ends of seam. Turn the adjacent folded edges of the muslin squares over the raw edges of red square. Stitch with a blindstitch. (See Figure 1e.) Make each curve formed by turning folded edges to front identical to the others.

### To make rows

**1.** Make up 14 muslin units without the red center square. Make a row by hand-stitching these 14 units together along the short edges.

**2.** Next, add a red square to each unit, as described above. You will need 13 red squares.

**3.** Make up another row of 14 muslin units.

**4.** Join row 1 and row 2 along the long edge, using an overcast stitch.

**5.** Refer to Figure 2. Next, place a red square horizontally and vertically between joined muslin squares and repeat step 4 of "To Make a Square," on page 131.

**6.** Continue to make rows of 14 folded muslin squares with red squares between until you have a total of 18 rows with 14 squares in each.

### To finish

I did not include backing, batting, or borders, because once the squares are stitched together, the quilt is finished on front and back. If you prefer a continuous, solid backing, you will need 3½ yards of fabric. Cut the fabric in half and stitch the 2 pieces together to create a large enough piece for the back. (See page 13 for backing details.) With wrong side up, spread out backing with seam running horizontally rather than vertically. Center top on backing and trim backing so it is ¼ inch larger than the top all around.

Turn raw edges under ¼ inch and press. With wrong sides together, slip-stitch or machine-stitch all around edges. From the front of the quilt, tack here and there to hold the backing in place.

As you can see, once the Cathedral Window squares are stitched together, the quilt is complete. There is no more quilting to be done, so perhaps you won't feel this quilt is too big an undertaking after all.

**Cathedral Window Quilt**

Figure 1. To make a square

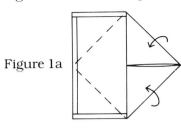

Figure 1a

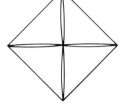

Figure 1b

Figure 1c

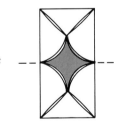

Figure 1d

Figure 1e

Figure 2. To make a row

# "54-40 or Fight" Quilt

I'm not sure where the title for this quilt came from, but it's actually a variation on a traditional star pattern. At first glance you might wonder who would spend the time to make such a complex-looking quilt. Believe it or not, Margaret Detmer made this as a first quilting project!

Maggie began by cutting up tiny pieces of colored paper to create the finished design on paper. (She still has this, framed, as a reminder of the quilt's humble beginnings.) The decision to make this quilt came out of a class she took with Jeffrey Gutcheon, who taught his students how to experiment with darks and lights in order to create new patterns. The most dramatic aspect of this quilt is the way Maggie created circles with the placement of colors. The evenly spaced quilt design of concentric circles further emphasizes the circular quality of the design. Notice, too, the use of light-colored fabrics in the center of the quilt, with dark colors arranged around the outer edges.

Think of making this project one block at a time, and study the diagrams. Once you understand how this lovely quilt is put together, you'll be inspired to make it. Take the time to plan your colors carefully. It will be well worth the effort. Maggie said that she bought a variety of ¼-yard pieces to work out the color scheme for her wall hanging, which is 60 × 72 inches. This size will also fit a double or queen-size bed.

## Materials

*Note:* Yardages are figured for fabric 45 inches wide.

2 yards light fabric

2 yards medium fabric

2 yards dark fabric

3½ yards dark fabric for the backing and border (dark blue used here)

thin batting

cardboard for templates

## Directions

Trace pattern pieces and transfer to cardboard to make templates. (See page 14 for template details.)

*Cut the following from medium, dark, and light fabrics in approximately equal numbers:*

*Note:* All measurements include ¼-inch seam allowance.

     120 squares, each 5 × 5 inches. Cut each square into 2 triangles.

     120 squares, each 2½ × 2½ inches

     260 pieces from Template 1

     110 pieces from Template 2

Detail: "54-40 or Fight" Quilt

## "54-40 or Fight" Quilt

### Figure 1

Figure 1a

Figure 1b

Figure 1c

Figure 2. To make a block

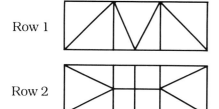

Row 1

Row 2

Row 3

**1.** With right sides facing and raw edges aligned, stitch 2 triangles of different color values together to make a square, as shown in Figure 1a. Open seams and press. Make 4, mixing dark, medium, and light colors.

**2.** With right sides facing and raw edges aligned, stitch 4 small squares (each 2½ × 2½ inches) together to make a larger square, as shown in Figure 1b. Open seams and press.

**3.** With right sides facing and raw edges aligned, stitch a piece cut from Template 1 to each side of a piece cut from Template 2 to make a square, as shown in Figure 1c. Open seams and press. Make 4, mixing dark, medium, and light colors.

### To make a block (Refer to Figure 2)

**1.** With right sides facing and raw edges aligned, stitch 3 of the squares together to make a row. Make 3 rows. Open seams and press.

**2.** Next, stitch all 3 rows together along the long edge to make a block. Open seams and press. Make 25 blocks.

### To make a half-block (Refer to Figure 3)

**1.** With right sides facing and raw edges aligned, stitch 2 pieces of different color values cut from Template 1 together to make a square, as shown in Figure 3a. Open seams and press. Make 2.

**2.** With right sides facing and raw edges aligned, stitch 2 small squares (each 2½ × 2½ inches) of different color values together as shown in Figure 3b. Open seams and press.

**3.** Join the 3 pieces together to make row 1 of Figure 3c.

**4.** Make 2 pieces of Figure 1a and 1 piece of Figure 1c as directed above.

**5.** Join the 3 pieces together to make row 2 of Figure 3c.

**6.** With right sides facing and raw edges aligned, join the 2 rows along one long edge. Open seams and press. Make 10.

### To make rows (Refer to Figure 4)

**1.** With right sides facing and raw edges aligned, stitch 2 blocks together along one side. Open seams and press.

**2.** Next, join 3 more blocks to make a row of 5 blocks, as shown in Figure 4a. Open seams and press. Make 5 rows.

**3.** With right sides facing and raw edges aligned, join 5 half-blocks to make a row, as shown in Figure 4b. Make 2.

### Figure 3

Figure 3a

Figure 3b

Row 1

Row 2

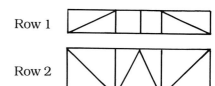

Figure 3c

### To join rows

**1.** With right sides facing and raw edges aligned, stitch the row made from half-blocks to the top edge of a full block row. Open seams and press.

**2.** Continue to join all rows in this way, ending with the remaining row of half-blocks. (See Figure 5.) Open seams and press.

### To quilt

**1.** If you want to create a quilt design of concentric circles, you'll need a compass to draw the circles on the quilt top. An alternative is to use a yardstick to create an overall grid of evenly spaced lines, 1 inch apart, to follow. (See page 17 for details.) Or simply skip to step 6 and quilt along all seam lines, as we have with many of the other projects.

**2.** Cut the backing fabric in half so that you have 2 pieces, each 1¾ yards long. (See page 13 for backing details.)

**3.** With right sides facing and raw edges aligned, stitch the backing fabric together along one long edge. Open seams and press.

**4.** With wrong side facing up, spread out backing with seam running horizontally rather than vertically. Center the batting and the quilt top on the backing. Trim the backing fabric 1 inch larger than quilt top all around. Trim the batting to same size as quilt top.

**5.** Beginning at the center and working outward in a sunburst pattern, take long basting stitches through all 3 layers.

**6.** Using small running stitches, quilt along all marked lines. (See page 16 for quilting details.)

**7.** When quilting is complete, remove all basting stitches.

### To finish

**1.** Fold the backing edges over ¼ inch all around and press.

**2.** Fold the edges over ¼ inch again onto the front of the quilt top and press. This creates a ½-inch border all around the wall hanging.

**3.** Slip-stitch the backing edge to the quilt top to finish.

### "54-40 or Fight" Quilt

Figure 4

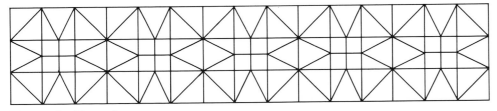

Figure 4a. To make a row

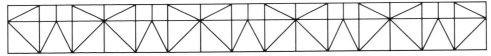

Figure 4b. Joining half-blocks to make a row

**"54-40 or Fight" Quilt**

Figure 5

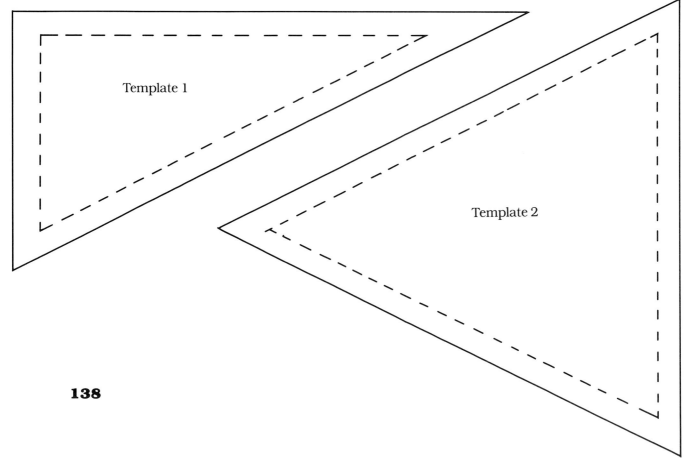

Template 1

Template 2

138

# Polka-Dot Quilt

Jon and I are familiar with a wide variety of quilt patterns, but this polka-dot design is one we've never seen before. When we saw this antique quilt hanging in a friend's contemporary home, we knew we had to include it in this book. The bold, graphic quality of the design is amazingly modern-looking, even though the quilt design is a variation of a traditional pattern similar to Drunkard's Path.

This 70 × 90-inch quilt was created by piecing curves. We've figured out the directions for making it in order to give our readers the opportunity to re-create it as a quilt or wall hanging. The faded red fabric of the original gives it a special quality that your quilt can acquire only in time. You can certainly do as the original quiltmaker did, and hand-quilt the entire project. Years from now, when the fabric has faded and the quilt has become worn and soft from use, you may have a prized heirloom among your possessions.

## Materials

4 yards red fabric
4 yards white fabric
4 yards red *or* white material for backing
batting
tracing paper
cardboard for templates
yardstick
soft pencil

## Directions

**1.** Trace each pattern piece and transfer to cardboard to make templates. (See page 14 for template details.) Cut out each one.
**2.** On the wrong side of the red fabric, trace 504 times around Template 1. On the wrong side of the white fabric, trace 252 times around Template 2. Cut out all pieces.

*To make a block*

**1.** Fold curved edges of all red pieces under ¼ inch and press. (See page 14 for details on sewing curves.)
**2.** Pin one red piece over the curved seam allowance on each side of the white pieces to make a square, as shown in Figure 1.
**3.** Join the pieces together with small slip-stitches around all curves. Press. This is one block. Make a total of 252.

*To make rows*

*Row 1*

**1.** With right sides facing and raw edges aligned, join 2 blocks together, as shown in row 1 of Figure 2. Open seams and press.

**2.** Continue joining blocks in this way until you have a row of 14 blocks, arranged as shown for row 1 in Figure 2. Make 9 rows.

*Row 2*

**1.** With right sides facing and raw edges aligned, join 14 blocks, arranged as shown for row 2 in Figure 2.

**2.** Open seams and press. Repeat to make 9 rows.

*To join rows* (Refer to Figure 3)

**1.** With right sides facing and raw edges aligned, stitch row 1 to row 2 along the long edge. Open seams and press.

**2.** Continue joining rows in this way, alternating row 1 and row 2. Open seams and press.

*To quilt*

You can do the quilting as we have on most of the other projects in this book, by taking small running stitches on either side of the seams. Or follow the original design and hand-quilt in an overall pattern of diagonal lines across the entire quilt top. (See page 17.)

**1.** Cut batting ½ inch smaller than quilt top all around.

**2.** Cut backing fabric in half so that there are 2 pieces, each 2 yards long. (See page 13 for backing details.)

**3.** With right sides facing and raw edges aligned, stitch the 2 pieces together along one long edge to create the backing fabric. Open seams and press. With wrong side facing up, spread out backing with seam running horizontally rather than vertically. Trim to same size as quilt top.

**4.** Starting in the center and working outward in a sunburst pattern, baste the top, batting, and backing together with long basting stitches through all 3 layers.

You should use white thread on the white fabric and red on the red circles. This means you'll have to change thread back and forth as you work, or quilt all white areas, then all red areas.

**5.** Thread needle with a length of approximately 18 inches. Beginning from the center and working outward, follow all marked lines and take small running stitches through all 3 layers. (See page 16 for hand-quilting details.) Do not stitch into seam allowance around edges.

*To finish*

**1.** When all quilting is complete, remove all basting stitches.

**2.** Fold the raw edge of the quilt top under ¼ inch and press. Turn the backing edges to the inside ¼ inch and press.

**3.** Stitch together with a slip-stitch or machine-stitch all around.

## Polka-Dot Quilt

Figure 1. To make a block

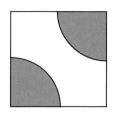

Figure 2. To make rows

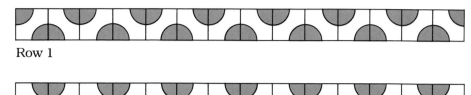

Row 1

Row 2

Figure 3. To join rows

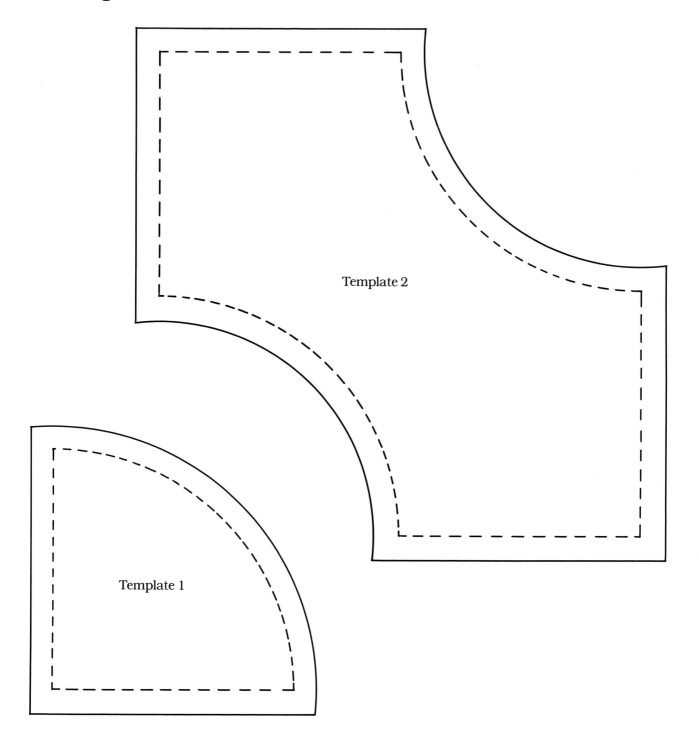

Template 2

Template 1

# Index

For information on how you can have
**Better Homes and Gardens**
delivered to your door, write to:
Mr. Robert Austin,
P.O. Box 4536, Des Moines, IA 50336.